Coaching
In A Week

Matt Somers is the UK's leading trainer of managers as coaches. His training programmes, books, articles and seminars have helped thousands of managers achieve outstanding results through their people. He runs programmes on an 'open' and 'in company' basis for coaches of all levels of ability and experience. Matt understands that people are working with their true potential locked away, and shows how coaching provides a simple yet elegant key to this lock.

For more information, go to www.mattsomers.com

I was introduced to coaching by Sir John Whitmore in 1995. Much of what follows here was inspired by that experience, and I can only hope that this small book inspires others to take up the coaching challenge in a similar way.

Teach Yourself®

Coaching
In A Week

Matt Somers

First published in Great Britain in 2002 by Hodder & Stoughton. An Hachette UK company.

First published in US in 2012 by The McGraw-Hill Companies, Inc.

This revised, updated edition published in 2016 by John Murray Learning

This edition published in US in 2016 by Quercus

Copyright © Matt Somers 2002, 2012, 2016

British Library Cataloguing in Publication Data: a catalogue record for this title is available from the British Library.

Library of Congress Catalog Card Number: on file.

Paperback ISBN 978 1 473 60940 2

Ebook ISBN 978 1 444 15906 6

1

Typeset by Cenveo® Publisher Services.

Printed and bound in Great Britain by CPI Group (UK) Ltd., Croydon, CR0 4YY.

John Murray Learning policy is to use papers that are natural, renewable and recyclable products and made from wood grown in sustainable forests. The logging and manufacturing processes are expected to conform to the environmental regulations of the country of origin.

John Murray Learning
Carmelite House
50 Victoria Embankment
London EC4Y 0DZ
www.hodder.co.uk

Also available
in ebook

Contents

Introduction

In recent years the idea of coaching and the role of coach have made the journey from the sports field, via Human Resources, to become part of everyday managerial life. The terms 'coach' and 'coaching' have become common, even trendy, but both are widely misunderstood. If you ask anyone to define the word 'coach', you will get a wide variety of responses.

Some kind of involvement in coaching is now part of most people's experience at work. Managers are expected to coach their team members, irrespective of whether assigned coaches are also offering coaching. Team members, for their part, are expected to welcome coaching from all quarters and engage fully in the conversations it requires.

Coaching is ultimately about raising the levels of human performance and, as such, has connections with teaching, training, counselling and mentoring. However, there are subtle but important differences that we need to understand.

In essence, coaching has two main facets. First, it is **performance focused**, which means that it is concerned with helping individuals perform tasks to the best of their ability. Second, it is **person centred**, which means that the individuals being coached are seen as having the important insights.

Fundamentally, then, coaching is about drawing *out*, not putting *in*. It is not the pushing down of advice from the wise to the less wise; it is more about helping people derive wisdom from their own experiences in their own way.

By using coaching, we can tap into the huge reserves of talent and potential that lie dormant in most people. As managers, we can develop people without having to rely on passing on our own skills and knowledge, which may already be out of date. Using our skills in coaching, we can help our people access their ability without needing more than a basic grasp of the technicalities of their role.

Without an ability to coach, we are reliant upon the tired old methods of teaching and instruction. These methods are proving increasingly ineffective in the world of constant change to which we are all having to adjust.

This book aims to give you enough knowledge and appreciation of coaching that you can begin to develop your own approach. A fact-check at the end of each chapter will help you do this. Over the course of one week you will look in depth at the skills and techniques involved in becoming an effective coach. The first chapter, 'Sunday', explains what coaching is (and is not) and how it compares with other ways of developing people. From Monday to Friday you will learn how you, as a manager, can offer coaching to your team, and on Saturday you will look at how you can make coaching an integral part of people management and development within your organization.

To learn more about the practical issues involved in setting up and running your own formal and informal coaching sessions, there is a further chapter called 'Coaching in practice' on my website, at www.mattsomers.com/extrachapter

Further information is also available from:
Matt Somers Coaching Skills Training
The Old Coach House
Castle Eden
County Durham
England
Tel: 01429 839 266

Matt Somers

SUNDAY

What is coaching?

When most people think about coaching, they imagine a sports coach shouting and yelling at the players, trying to help them succeed without being directly involved in the field of play.

In sport, the role of the coach is crucial to help people perform at their peak. Even the most accomplished sportspeople, such as Rory McIlroy or Serena Williams, still gain huge benefits from a good relationship with their coach. Few of these coaches were gifted performers themselves; their skills lie in getting the best out of other people.

Looking at coaching in this way, we can see that there is great benefit to be had from having people in organizations with the skills and abilities to draw the best out of others.

If it were possible for *everyone* in an organization to improve their performance by as little as 1 or 2 per cent, the results would be staggering. Modest personal change and improvement can combine to make a massive difference to the organization as a whole.

Today we will develop our understanding of coaching by looking at:

- some common myths about coaching
- the differences between coaching and other ways of developing people.

Coaching for development

Coaching is the practice of supporting an individual through a process of achieving a goal or solving a problem. Many organizations are now taking the power of coaching seriously and appointing people to the specific role of coach. While managers may have the skills and abilities to coach well, they are often preoccupied with more task-oriented matters and can struggle to find the time to coach effectively.

Increasingly, we are able to tap into coaching outside our organizations. Many small consultancies are now offering **executive coaching**. This is where top-level managers in organizations can have regular weekly or monthly sessions with a trained coach to help them work through their current issues. It can often be valuable to have a coach who does not work in the organization and who is, therefore, not involved in the same issues.

Similarly, many people are now seeking the services of **personal coaches** to help them work through personal problems, achieve goals and strike an effective work and life balance.

Whatever the context, we can see that coaching is intended to give one individual the means to help another move forward and develop in some way.

Coaching myths

Since the concept of coaching is often misunderstood, it is perhaps not surprising that many myths have sprung up around the subject. Can you see any truth in the following, for example?

- 'Everything's fine; we don't really have any problems and so we don't need coaching.'
- 'I'm not a manager or team leader so I don't have anyone to coach.'
- 'I haven't time to coach.'
- 'I can't coach – I have no expertise in the underlying subject.'
- 'I went on a course about this, but then it was called "feedback". That's all coaching really is.'
- 'This is just a fancy new name for what I've been doing for years – training people!'

Everything's fine; we don't really have any problems and so we don't need coaching

Many people believe that coaching is about putting wrong things right. They would argue that things must be pretty poor in an organization if it needs armies of people to solve other people's problems. If coaching is required, then it should be a short-term solution and the coaches should move on when things have been sorted out.

I'm not a manager or team leader so I don't have anyone to coach

Already we can see that coaching is a people development tool. By definition, that means we must have people to coach. What, then, is the point of developing good coaching skills if we do not currently operate as a manager, supervisor or team leader and do not have any people reporting to us?

I haven't time to coach

We now know that there is more to coaching than at first meets the eye. If we think for a moment that a typical team will have at least six to eight people working in it, then we can begin to see that the team leader's task is almost hopeless.

If six to eight people all want coaching every six weeks or so, in sessions lasting up to an hour, how would we do any work?

I can't coach – I have no expertise in the underlying subject

How can we coach somebody to do something we cannot do ourselves? How can we keep up with all the changes in the ways that people do their jobs? How can we expect people to take us seriously as managers if we are not prepared or able to do what we ask them to do?

I went on a course about this, but then it was called 'feedback'. That's all coaching really is

For many people, coaching is something that happens as part of an organization's performance management or appraisal system. In some organizations, coaches have been known to sit behind a colleague while they are dealing with a customer, and make notes on the things they did well or badly. Usually, the individual and the coach then retire to a quiet area where the coach can run through the list and make suggestions for improvement.

This is just a fancy new name for what I've been doing for years – training people!

Can we really see any daylight between coaching and other methods of developing people? Coaching is ultimately about making people better at what they do, but then so are teaching, training, mentoring and counselling.

> *'Those who cannot change their minds cannot change anything.'*
>
> George Bernard Shaw, playwright

Let us now complete a simple self-assessment to see whether you feel that these statements are myths or not. Make a note of your responses or put a tick in the box you feel most comfortable with.

Self-assessment

	This is true	This is a myth
Everything's fine; we don't really have any problems and so we don't need coaching.	❏	❏
I'm not a manager or team leader so I don't have anyone to coach.	❏	❏
I haven't time to coach.	❏	❏
I can't coach – I have no expertise in the underlying subject.	❏	❏
I went on a course about this, but then it was called 'feedback'. That's all coaching really is.	❏	❏
This is just a fancy new name for what I've been doing for years – training people!	❏	❏

We will revisit these statements again on Friday, after we have looked at coaching in more depth.

Coaching compared

We can begin to develop our understanding of coaching by considering how it compares with other ways of developing people. Specifically, let us consider the following:

- coaching and teaching
- coaching and training
- coaching and mentoring
- coaching and counselling.

Coaching and teaching

We know from our own experience at school that teaching tends to be delivered to groups, following a predetermined lesson plan and with people of mixed abilities developing their understanding as best they can.

Of course, teaching can be given on a one-to-one basis and there are countless people who have benefited from being taught or tutored in this way. However, the dominant party in the teacher–pupil relationship is the teacher. The teacher will be concerned with passing on knowledge, facts and wisdom and, as pupils, we usually take a passive role and try to absorb them. We have little scope to set or follow our own agenda and we have to try to interpret what the teacher is saying and make sense of it against our own experience.

Coaching, on the other hand, is more often than not delivered one to one. It is the person being coached – often called the coachee – who sets the agenda and decides on the issue to be considered. As coaches, we are not there to provide input or advice or to tell the coachee how we would do things. Instead, our role is to probe and encourage and help the coachee make sense of things for him- or herself.

This can be a difficult concept to grasp and a comparison is useful here. When we get up in the morning we usually pad across the hallway to the bathroom and begin the mammoth task of making ourselves look presentable. For some, this may mean dragging a razor across their face and a comb through their hair, while others may concentrate on applying

SUNDAY

MONDAY

TUESDAY

WEDNESDAY

THURSDAY

FRIDAY

SATURDAY

make-up and hairspray. All of these activities would be almost impossible without our trusty friend the bathroom mirror.

But does the mirror say, 'Ooh, I wouldn't do it like that,' or 'That's not how we usually shave here,' or 'You've never done your hair like that before'? Of course not! Nevertheless, the mirror does help us make sense of what is going on and achieve our aim, which is in this case to look presentable before we face the world.

When we are coaching, we are trying to perform the same function. The best coaches will hold up a 'mirror' so that people can develop a deep sense of self-awareness. When people are highly self-aware, they have more choices about how to move issues forward.

Coaching and training

Bearing this in mind, we can see that coaching is different from training. Training is concerned with helping people to perform, of course, but again it is centred on the trainer and the subject matter, not on the individual.

Coaching and mentoring

Coaches and mentors share many of the same skills and abilities, but they are usually different people. A mentor is typically a senior person of greater experience who is invited to take us 'under their wing' and let us benefit from their wisdom. If it is coaching we want, however, we are probably best advised to avoid a more experienced person who may be tempted to persuade us to 'do it their way'.

Given that we can now see how coaching is wholly concerned with drawing out and not putting in, we can also see how it is possible for anyone with the right skills to coach us – their position in the organization is irrelevant.

Coaching and counselling

When we consider how coaching compares with counselling, we need to think about the limitations of coaching. Coaching in organizations is concerned with helping people to perform well in their jobs, not with dealing with deep-rooted problems from the past.

11

It is possible that we might uncover some painful or personal issues as we coach, so we need to know when to bring in the appropriate expertise. Most effective coaches are not trained counsellors or therapists, but they can still deliver excellent coaching support.

In short, the best coaches have a simple philosophy:

> **'The brain with the problem is the one with the solution.'**

Choosing the right approach

Arguably, this exercise of comparison is academic. Do we really need to worry what method is used to develop people, provided they are being developed? The short answer is no, but we do need to understand the unique qualities of coaching so that we can use it with choice and with greater care.

In reality, good coaches draw on all of these different approaches as they work with individuals. They will not be concerned about whether they are coaching or teaching at any one point in time. However, they will be concerned with using the right approach based on the needs of the individual and the demands of the situation.

I KNOW I HAVE THE ANSWER SOMEWHERE

Coaches work on this basis in the certain belief that people have vast reserves of potential that are rarely used, and that their job is to draw it out.

A coaching philosophy

We cannot prove human nature; we can only form our own view. One of the most accessible pieces of theory on this point was provided by Douglas McGregor when he described the idea that managers view their people in one or the other of two contrasting categories. He labelled these Theory X and Theory Y.

Theory X	Theory Y
People are lazy and dislike work	Work is a natural part of life
People must be coerced or threatened with punishment	People will exercise self-direction
People avoid responsibility	People accept responsibility under the right conditions
People are motivated mainly by money	People are motivated by achievement, recognition and job satisfaction

These two theories are really the extreme ends of the same spectrum. Most of us would admit to feeling a mixture of these views about some people some of the time. However, successful coaching means taking a positive view of human nature and the capabilities of people and, as such, it is aligned with Theory Y.

SUNDAY

MONDAY

TUESDAY

WEDNESDAY

THURSDAY

FRIDAY

SATURDAY

Summary

Today has been about establishing an understanding of the coaching concept. We have outlined the basic philosophy of coaching, which is about recognizing that people are not empty vessels into which knowledge and skills must be poured; rather, they are seedlings that require careful nurturing and support.

In this chapter we have begun to develop an approach to coaching in keeping with these ideas:

● Coaching in organizations is broadly similar to coaching in sport, in that the primary concern is to perform better and develop people's abilities.

● Coaching can be interpreted in different ways, and the concept is often misunderstood.

● Coaching shares many characteristics with teaching, counselling and training, but it has some subtle but important differences.

● Effective coaching allows people to develop their sense of self-awareness so that they begin to see their problems and concerns with greater clarity.

The remainder of the week will be concerned with developing our understanding and practical skills, so that we can become excellent coaches for the benefit of others and ourselves.

Tomorrow we will look more closely at coaching in the workplace and consider how we can build coaching into the set of management skills we already have.

Fact-check [answers at the back]

1. What is the purpose of coaching an individual?
a) To solve the other person's problems for them ❏
b) To advise the person on the best way forward ❏
c) To help the person move forward in some way ❏
d) To provide one-to-one training ❏

2. What does being performance focused mean?
a) Helping individuals to perform tasks to the best of their ability ❏
b) Obsessing over goals and targets ❏
c) Placing the needs of the organization first ❏
d) Doing whatever is necessary to beat the competition ❏

3. What is the person being coached normally referred to as?
a) The coachee ❏
b) The underperformer ❏
c) The problem ❏
d) The client ❏

4. What would sitting with someone and pointing out their mistakes be best thought of as?
a) Coaching ❏
b) Training ❏
c) Mentoring ❏
d) Largely unhelpful ❏

5. What issues do managers face around coaching, even when they have the skills and abilities to coach?
a) They generally can't be bothered ❏
b) They struggle to find the time to coach effectively ❏
c) They worry about doing more harm than good ❏
d) They think they should leave coaching to trained professionals ❏

6. Complete this phrase: 'The brain with the problem...
a) ...is the brain we shouldn't have hired' ❏
b) ...is the one with the solution' ❏
c) ...must have a problem in the brain' ❏
d) ...is in need of my advice' ❏

7. Why do the best coaches hold up a 'mirror' to coachees?
a) So that they can see their flaws ❏
b) So that they can reflect on where they are going wrong ❏
c) So that they can look at things from a different angle ❏
d) So that they can develop a deep sense of self-awareness ❏

8. What does McGregor's Theory Y state?
a) People are lazy and dislike work ❏
b) People accept responsibility under the right conditions ❏
c) People are motivated mainly by money ❏
d) People need to be threatened with punishment ❏

9. What is the main difference between coaching and counselling?
a) Counselling involves giving lots of advice ❏
b) Coaching starts in the present, irrespective of what has happened in the past ❏
c) They require completely different skill sets ❏
d) They are spelled differently ❏

10. Who would a mentor in an organization typically be?
a) A senior person with greater experience ❏
b) An outside consultant ❏
c) A person with too much time on their hands ❏
d) A new starter ❏

MONDAY

The manager as coach

On Sunday we saw that, with the appropriate skills, it is possible for any person to coach another and that therefore line managers are ideally placed to coach their team members. However, since we, as managers, have a host of other responsibilities to attend to, this might make it difficult to coach as often or as effectively as we might like.

We have already said that some organizations solve this problem by appointing people to a specific coaching role. However, in many workplaces this is simply not feasible and it is usually much more effective to ensure that all managers and team leaders are equipped with good coaching skills.

The trick is for us to understand and acknowledge some of the tensions created by acting as coach and manager to the same group of people.

Today we look at the following:

- barriers to coaching
- coaching and communication
- the communication spectrum
- where coaching fits in
- communicating for development.

SUNDAY

MONDAY

TUESDAY

WEDNESDAY

THURSDAY

FRIDAY

SATURDAY

Barriers to coaching

Let us look at some specific issues that may prevent you, as a manager, from offering coaching:

- 'I also have a range of other tasks to attend to.'
- 'I might have to discipline the same people.'
- 'I might not be able to give them what they want.'
- 'There might be more pressing issues.'

I also have a range of other tasks to attend to

In our roles as managers we have many demands on our time. We probably have to allocate and distribute the team's work, monitor budgets, keep records, attend to quality control, and so on. For most of us it is impossible to do everything and so we prioritize, trying to attend to what we consider the most important jobs first.

Unfortunately, this can lead to 'short-termism' and constant firefighting, and it can mean that coaching and training take a back seat. We tell ourselves that coaching and training are important and that we will do some when we have finished all these other things. But tomorrow never comes and our in-trays fill up with more urgent or important stuff. The coaching is left for another day, and so it goes on.

The great irony is that we can break this vicious circle only by investing time in training and coaching the team, ensuring that, increasingly, they are able to take on more tasks. This frees the manager to do more coaching and creates a virtuous circle instead.

I might have to discipline the same people

This is undoubtedly true and needs to be considered when establishing an effective coaching relationship. As coaches, we are concerned primarily with helping others to learn, and we need the coachees to feel completely comfortable talking through work-related issues with us. A good coaching relationship is founded on trust.

We must trust our team members to work towards their potential and they must trust that we, as their coaches, will keep anything that is discussed during a coaching session confidential.

We need to explain to people that, as managers, we wear 'different hats' and that we coach with the utmost sincerity; our concern is to work together to identify improvements in performance.

Other management processes, such as promotion panels or disciplinary matters, should be handled separately from coaching sessions to avoid confusion between the roles.

Because coaching works only against a background of trust, which often takes time to build, we may have to wait patiently for the coaching sessions to develop to a point where people feel really comfortable in talking about things they would like to address. Happily, coaching is an effective way of generating trust quickly. People soon see that the good coach genuinely wants to help them to reach their potential.

I might not be able to give them what they want

Some managers worry that their staff might 'hijack' coaching sessions and use them to ask for all sorts of expensive or irrelevant training courses or funded education programmes. These same managers fear that, by turning down such requests, they are seen as insincere and as not really taking their coaching role seriously.

Once again, trust is important here, as is clearly defining the purpose of coaching at the outset. We need to make sure that our team members realize that coaching is about helping them move forward and about exploring ways of achieving this, but that coaching does not take place in a vacuum. In other words while, as a coach, we wish to support a person's development, quite obviously we will need to balance this against a range of other factors such as other team members' needs, budgets, timescales and so on.

 We may be unable to grant every request that emerges from a coaching session, but this is no reason not to coach in the first place.

There might be more pressing issues

Later on we will look at structuring a coaching session. This will show that the most effective coaching happens when the individual sets the agenda because this is in keeping with the notion that coaching should raise awareness and generate responsibility.

However, many managers are at a loss if their own view of current performance issues differs from those of the team members. Again, we must acknowledge that, although a possibility, this is not a reason to avoid coaching.

It is important to recognize that we cannot hide behind coaching to avoid a difficult performance issue. If there is a need to 'tell it like it is' or to give someone some pointed feedback, then that is what managers must do. Furthermore, managers should do so openly and honestly and not pretend they are delivering a coaching session for the other person's benefit.

It is important that we understand these factors when we consider the role of the manager as coach. None of the problems mentioned is insurmountable and, provided we are aware of them, none presents any real barrier to effective coaching.

Coaching and communication

So far, we have considered some of the difficulties in defining coaching with any precision and of incorporating coaching into our general management role.

We can now turn our attention to understanding the application of coaching so that we may begin to coach the people in our teams (and ourselves!) towards higher levels of performance.

A useful starting point is to consider coaching as one type of communication and to see how it fits in with the typical management communication that most of us will recognize.

The communication spectrum

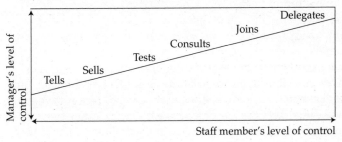

This diagram illustrates that there is a variety of management communication styles and that they vary depending on the amount of control the manager takes compared with his or her staff.

Let us now consider the relative advantages and disadvantages of each.

Tells

Managers who use this style prefer to manage by command and control; they are sometimes referred to as autocrats. This style means that the manager can exercise great control because he or she can be sure that work is carried out in accordance with their detailed instructions. This style also has the benefit of ensuring a consistent approach and is likely to absorb far less time than having a meeting arranged and sitting around while everyone in the team has their say.

However, people who work for managers like this often complain of feeling put upon and unappreciated. They may feel frustrated at not being given a chance to have their say, and they can end up following instructions to the letter and exercising little, if any, initiative.

From the manager's point of view, this style does not really allow the team members to use their creativity and experience, and it also assumes that the manager has experienced all the problems and knows all the answers. Increasingly, this is not the case.

Sells

This is a slightly softer style than *Tells*; there is at least some attempt to involve the members of the team. Here, the manager still devises the plans and makes the decisions but also considers the needs of the team by trying to sell the benefits of his or her suggestions. However, actions are still based on his or her suggestions, without much scope for team contributions. Moreover, if the team do not initially buy a suggestion, it is likely that the manager will resort to *Tell* and insist that the team do as they are asked, whether they like it or not.

Tests

The difference between *Sells* and *Tests* is slight. It is really about the manager approaching the team with an idea and seeing what their reaction is. If the initial suggestion is received with enthusiasm, this style of manager is likely to relinquish control to a fair degree and allow the team to undertake the work under his or her guidance. If the initial suggestion is resisted, the manager may decide to revisit certain decisions and see if a more positive way forward can be formulated.

Consults

By now we have reached a point where control is evenly split. The manager is still taking a lead role but will be keen to involve the team as much as possible and may prefer to avoid making decisions until after the team has had a chance to discuss matters. This can be a problem because decisions may be delayed until everyone in the team has had a chance to have their say. It is also far from certain that decisions made in this way will be any better than if the manager had made them on his or her own. It has been said that a camel is only a horse designed by a committee where everyone insisted on having their bit included!

Joins

Some managers prefer a style of communication that plays down their role as the leader of the team. They like to position themselves as just one of the group, whose opinions and ideas are no more valid than anyone else's. This can create a dynamic team atmosphere and make people feel highly valued.

It is likely that groups managed in this way will produce a range of creative ideas and largely relieve the manager of the burden of control. However, as with *Consults*, this style uses a lot of time and may be inappropriate when a speedy, emphatic decision is needed.

Delegates

At the other end of the spectrum is the management style of *Delegates*. This means that the manager explains the requirements of a task and sets the rules and deadlines. However, he or she then leaves the team or the individual to achieve the desired results as they see fit.

This quite clearly emphasizes trust and faith in others, but cannot be done without some thought. Managers need to know their team well enough to decide who should do what, and they must never delegate accountability. In other words, if it goes wrong, the manager carries the can – it is part of being a manager!

When considering styles of management communication, a common mistake is to think that one style is necessarily correct. Each has its advantages and disadvantages. The most effective managers adapt their style to reflect the needs of the situation and the needs of the person with whom they are communicating. For example, if a fire alarm sounded as you are reading this, it would be absurd to arrange a meeting to discuss options for evacuating the building. What is needed is someone to take the lead and ensure that people are moved to safety quickly and in accordance with the laid down procedures.

Similarly, a new person on the team will need a period of close monitoring and some instruction before they have built up the knowledge and experience required for delegated tasks.

Where does coaching fit in?

So how does all this relate to coaching, and where would we place coaching on the spectrum? Some argue that coaching is all about empowering others and therefore it must sit 'right of centre' towards delegation. However, we can see that coaching may not belong on this line at all because it represents almost a philosophy of communication rather than a style. In many ways, coaching is a means of adopting the advantages of each of the other styles, while minimizing the disadvantages.

Good coaches do not fear loss of control; they know that the people they coach will have formulated their plans and ideas in their presence. Thus, the coach has the ability to warn against a certain course of action if it is against the rules or likely to cause problems. Also, we have seen that coaching is an effective way for managers to build trust in their teams. They can resort to *Tell* when the situation demands it, without worrying about the team being uncooperative or becoming disillusioned.

Communicating for development

Up to now we have considered the merits of various communication styles in a general context. What about when we need to communicate with another to help them develop?

It seems that *Tell* is dominant here and perhaps this is because most of us are conditioned to learn this way at school. Pupils sit in rows of desks or tables while the teacher tells them what they need to do and how to do it. Lessons consist of being told what we need to know. But this does not always work. Try explaining to someone how to do up a tie or lace a training shoe without showing them – it is almost impossible. To do so requires us, first, to understand exactly the process that needs to be done and then to find the language to convey that process to another person in a way they can understand.

The modern world of work is changing so fast that we can no longer be certain that the ways and methods we once used to become successful will be valid for the next generation. Solving today's problems with yesterday's solutions is a big risk.

Furthermore, people do not retain a great deal of learning when they have only ever been told what to do. How many managers have you heard yelling, 'If I've told you once, I've told you a thousand times!', or 'How many times do I have to tell you?'

Coaching presents a way of dealing with these problems because it is concerned with drawing out rather than putting in. It therefore enables people to learn in their own way and at their own speed. In this way we get learning and development that sticks, in the same way that learning to swim or ride a bicycle stays with us.

> *'Tell me and I forget,*
> *Show me and I remember,*
> *Involve me and I understand.'*
>
> Chinese proverb

 TIP *Coaching is the best way to involve people in their own learning.*

Summary

Today we have seen that we face a challenge in adding coaching to our toolbox of management skills. Our other responsibilities mean that it is not always easy to coach our teams, and so we need to work on building coaching into our existing communication style. We also saw that our communication style will be influenced by the needs of the situation and by the needs of the person on the receiving end of our communication.

Your own beliefs and values about management will heavily influence your communication style. You will need to think about how much confidence you have in your team members and how you have been influenced by the managers you have worked for in the past. You will also need to think through your own beliefs about leadership and the sort of leader you would like to be.

One thing is certain: by reading this book and being open to the ideas and techniques of coaching, you have already begun to realize that an inescapable part of your job is to get results through others. The better they are able to perform their roles, the higher your own chances of personal success will be.

Tomorrow we will start to explore how to go about coaching, by looking at the underlying principles.

SUNDAY
MONDAY
TUESDAY
WEDNESDAY
THURSDAY
FRIDAY
SATURDAY

Fact-check [answers at the back]

1. How does the old Chinese proverb that starts, 'Tell me and...' continue?
   a) I obey ❏
   b) I remember ❏
   c) I resist ❏
   d) I forget ❏

2. If you put off coaching in order to get more work done, what do you create?
   a) A happy and fulfilled team ❏
   b) A virtuous circle ❏
   c) A vicious circle ❏
   d) A warm sense of accomplishment ❏

3. When we learned to ride a bike or to swim, why did the learning stick?
   a) We learned in our own way at our own speed ❏
   b) We were taught by accomplished swimmers and cyclists ❏
   c) We would otherwise have been punished for not learning ❏
   d) We were given financial rewards for learning ❏

4. What is a good coaching relationship founded on?
   a) Fear ❏
   b) Trust ❏
   c) Power ❏
   d) The meeting room on the ground floor ❏

5. Where would we place coaching on the communication spectrum?
   a) Alongside *Tells*, because coaching is about giving advice and guidance ❏
   b) Within *Consults*, because coaching is about deciding everything jointly ❏
   c) Nowhere. Coaching goes around the spectrum, not on it ❏
   d) Beside *Sells*, because coaches need to convince others of their expertise ❏

6. When does the most effective coaching happen?
   a) When the coach sets the agenda ❏
   b) When the coachee sets the agenda ❏
   c) When there is no agenda ❏
   d) When the HR Manager sets the agenda ❏

7. Which of these statements is true?
   a) Coaching means we can always avoid having to give difficult feedback ❏
   b) Coaching does not mean we won't ever have to give difficult feedback ❏
   c) Coaching means we can sometimes avoid having to give difficult feedback ❏
   d) Coaching means we can occasionally avoid having to give difficult feedback ❏

8. What are managers who 'tell' and prefer to manage by command and control sometimes referred to as?
a) Aristocrats ❏
b) Autocrats ❏
c) Dictators ❏
d) Mad ❏

9. Which of these statements is false?
a) As a manager who coaches, I might not always be able to give people what they want ❏
b) As a manager who coaches, I may sometimes have more pressing issues ❏
c) As a manager who coaches, I avoid having to discipline the team ❏
d) As a manager who coaches, I may sometimes have to discipline people ❏

10. What would solving today's problems with yesterday's solutions be?
a) Cheap and cost-effective ❏
b) Timely and efficient ❏
c) Good for the manager's ego ❏
d) A big risk ❏

TUESDAY

The key principles of coaching

Now that we know that the *Tell* style is somewhat ineffective when it comes to helping others learn and develop, we need to consider other ways to do this.

Perhaps we should demonstrate and *show* others what to do. This means we would have to be able to do all the team's jobs and keep up with any changes that happen to those jobs. Most managers are busy enough keeping abreast of developments in their own jobs, let alone those of their team.

If we cannot tell and we cannot show, all we can do is question. Bizarre though it may seem, one of the most powerful ways to coach another individual is to ask a series of questions, carefully designed to help them think for themselves. However, we need first to establish certain key principles in order for you to develop your own style over time, without having to refer back to the 'recipe'.

Today we will look at:

- the key qualities a coach needs
- how to identify and deal with performance gaps.

Asking questions

Normally, we ask questions because we want answers. However, the coach is concerned not with answers but with giving people an opportunity to think with greater clarity, so that they can formulate solutions or ideas that will work for them. For some, this requires a leap of faith since they need to accept that, almost invariably, the way towards performance improvement lies within.

Much of the remainder of this book will show you a detailed approach to constructing questions in a coaching session. You will then have the ability to coach in this way when you have finished reading.

We can start by looking at the qualities you will need to develop in order to become an effective coach.

Coaching qualities

We will consider the three essential qualities an effective coach needs: the right attitude, skills and knowledge.

Attitude

We have seen that coaches have a healthy attitude towards other people, demonstrated by the three main things they do in their coaching sessions.

First, they concentrate wholly on the people they coach in order to raise levels of **self-awareness**. Second, they use encouragement and support to make sure that the people they coach take **responsibility** for moving their own issues forward. Third, they are open and honest and genuinely want to see others succeed. In this way they quickly build strong relationships of **trust**.

Raising awareness

On Sunday we saw that looking in our bathroom mirror can raise our awareness of how we look, and we can use this information to improve our performance in 'looking good'. Just being aware of what is going on when we experience certain things is often all it takes to make improvements – it is a natural process.

Perhaps you have experienced the sensation of daydreaming while driving, to the extent that you cannot recall whether you have passed your turning or not. When this happens, it is because we are performing on 'autopilot'; in other words, we are not consciously aware of what we are doing. This situation can be remedied simply by raising awareness once more. The next time you are driving, concentrate on how often this daydreaming happens. Paradoxically, because of your awareness and concentration, it will not happen at all.

Generating responsibility

Coaches want people to take responsibility for tackling their own problems and developing their own abilities. Insecure managers will often get a sense of satisfaction from 'rescuing' other people.

It makes them feel good because they have helped someone out and they believe that the other person will feel good because they have passed their dilemma to somebody else.

But these same managers have massive pending trays, groaning under the weight of other people's problems. If we solve a problem for somebody once, the chances are they will come knocking on our door each time they have another one. When we take responsibility for someone else's situation, we have failed to develop that person and we have simply reinforced their sense of dependence. Over the long term this can lead to feelings of frustration and resentment.

Building trust

Finally, effective coaches see the virtuous circle of establishing trust. They realize that, by raising awareness and generating responsibility, they are providing people with a platform to perform at higher levels. As this happens, the coach's staff will develop a trust in the coaching process and, in turn, answer their coach's questions with deeper levels of honesty and candour. Our coaching will help them to become more self-aware and responsible and the effects will perpetuate.

 Always remember that raising awareness, generating responsibility and building trust are the key principles of effective coaching.

Skills

The two main skills of coaching are the ability to ask probing questions and the capacity for active listening.

Asking probing questions

We saw earlier that asking questions is essentially the way that we can help coachees to find their own solutions in their own way. A probing question is simply one that gets to the heart of the matter and, with this in mind, we are better off asking 'open' rather than 'closed' questions. An open question will begin with *Who*, *What*, *How*, *When*, and so on. It encourages the person responding to think carefully and to give a full reply.

A closed question, on the other hand, will tend to begin with *Did you*, *Can you*, *Will you*, and so forth. It normally gets a sharp yes or no response. This is unhelpful in a coaching conversation because it does not produce any sense of flow or rhythm and can often mean that the coach struggles to formulate the next question.

Closed questions also appear when a manager tries to use coaching as *Tell* or *Sell* in disguise and asks questions like 'Don't you think you ought to...?' and 'Wouldn't it be better if...?'

By using open questions, we can start with a broad 'How are things?' and then go deeper as the conversation progresses. We can end up with questions like 'How often each day would you find yourself being snappy with customers?' or 'How much time exactly would you need to complete the task?'

On Wednesday we shall look at a framework for asking questions to ensure that you are helping the people you coach to raise their levels of self-awareness and to take responsibility for any actions they need to implement.

Active listening

If we are going to put so much effort into framing questions in the right way, then it follows that we should be equally concerned with really listening to the responses we get. We need to employ the skill of active listening.

Listening happens at three levels:

The bottom level, **Superficial**, is what we do when we are hearing but not listening. We might have a conversation at a party and try to take an interest in what another guest is saying but really our attention is elsewhere, perhaps on some other conversation that we suspect would be far more interesting.

The problem is that we are only *hearing* what the other guest is saying, not listening, and so we often get confused, lose track of the conversation or end up having to ask them to repeat what they just said.

In a coaching session this would be extremely damaging. If we are only hearing superficially, because our mind is elsewhere, it will be reflected in our body language and the person being coached will know immediately. This will destroy any trust in the coaching relationship and make it unlikely that the coaching will result in any useful outcomes.

The next level, **Conversational**, is the sort of listening that most of us do most of the time. In conversational listening, we listen while our partners talk and vice versa. However, the danger is that, while the other person is talking, we are concentrating on making our next point, rather than truly focusing on what that person is saying.

This is quite a challenge when you start coaching because it can be hard to keep the questions flowing when you are trying to listen as well. It is better to pause and think of the next question when the person has finished speaking, rather than dwell on it when they are in full flow.

We must also watch out for the habit of finishing other people's sentences. Invariably, we do not pick the words they would have chosen for themselves and we end up only disrupting the flow of their thinking and making them feel hurried.

I'M A VERY GOOD LISTENER

It is clear that we need to work hard to reach the top level, **Active** listening. Put simply, active listening is about clearing our minds of all other distractions and really tuning in to what the other person is saying, with as much focus as we can muster. This is easier said than done and takes a great deal of time and practice to develop, but it is well worth the effort.

> **TIP** *We should try not to coach when we are in a hurry or preoccupied with something else. Neither should we run a coaching session in a noisy environment or one that is likely to get too hot or too cold. It is impossible to listen actively in such circumstances.*

Knowledge

In considering what knowledge is required to coach effectively, we need to look at two areas. We need to know, first, how much subject matter expertise we need and, second, how much we need to know about coaching itself.

Subject matter expertise

There is still some debate about whether coaches need a detailed knowledge of the matter in hand or underlying subject in order to coach another person effectively.

Some argue that it is impossible to coach without subject matter expertise because, without it, we cannot show another person what to do or give our advice or guidance. However, we have seen that telling people what to do is fraught with danger. We need to ask ourselves the following questions:

● Do I understand how I get results myself?
● Can I find a way to express that to another person?
● Will they remember what I have told them?

Unless we are clear about the answers, we cannot be sure that *telling* will work. We have also come to recognize that, these days, knowledge is out of date within a few months and it is risky to approach any situation with outdated knowledge. It is far better to coach in a way that allows other people to develop their own solutions and that encourages them to become self-reliant in the future.

In reality, we will probably have some background in the situations discussed during coaching sessions, but we should resist the temptation to jump in with our own quick-fix solutions.

Knowledge of coaching

This is a far more important area of knowledge for effective coaching and covers everything we have considered so far:

● what coaching is
● how managers can incorporate coaching in their own style
● the principles of awareness, responsibility and trust
● the skills of questioning and active listening.

Performance gaps

Ultimately, effective coaches use all their own knowledge, skills and attitude to work on the same aspects in the people they coach. If people are not performing to their potential, something will be missing in terms of their own knowledge, skills or attitude. In other words, there will be a performance gap.

Performance gaps in knowledge

Coaching is of little use when a person needs to develop their performance by acquiring knowledge; coaching cannot tease out what is not there.

SUNDAY
MONDAY
TUESDAY
WEDNESDAY
THURSDAY
FRIDAY
SATURDAY

For example, it would clearly be ridiculous for a driving instructor to take a pupil on a first lesson and ask, 'How might you press those pedals in sequence to bring about some forward movement?' The pupil would have no idea because, in the first instance, they need some input, some knowledge that they can begin to use and develop.

In such cases we are initially obliged to adopt a *Tell* style. However, we must recognize its drawbacks and look towards a coaching style as soon as the coachees have enough knowledge to develop their own learning.

Many coaches make the mistake of trying to coach where the development need is for knowledge. Invariably, the coaching session breaks down, leaving both parties feeling frustrated and confused by the coaching process.

Coaching can be useful to help people think for themselves about ways in which they might fill their knowledge gaps.

Performance gaps in skills

In any sphere of work we need not only a body of knowledge to be able to perform our job well but also a set of skills that allows us to put that knowledge to good use. The key to developing good skills is practice. If I wanted to develop my skills as a public speaker, I could read every book ever written on the subject, but I would not become a good public speaker until I had got on my feet and begun to practise the skills of positioning, hand gestures, speech variance, and so on.

Coaching can be very useful here. Although it cannot replace the time needed for practice, it can help people to decide exactly what their practice priorities should be and how they are going to get the most from any practice session.

In trying to develop my presentation skills, I might practise positioning my visual aids and asking the audience questions, because the books I read suggested that these were key aspects of successful presenting. However, my coach may help me realize that, in fact, my last presentation did not go as well as I hoped because I ran out of time and was rushed at the end. In this case it would be better for me to practise pacing my delivery and designing more flexible material.

Performance gaps in attitude

Coaching comes into its own as a development tool where individuals have a decent level of knowledge and skills but for some reason are not putting them to good use.

Of course, this may be because they have become disillusioned with the work or the organization and are looking for an opportunity to leave. If this is the case, it might be best for the parties to part company, and coaching could be offered to help people in this position decide on their next steps.

Quite often, though, people are not harnessing their knowledge and skills because they have lost sight of what they are trying to achieve. Alternatively, they may have some limiting beliefs that say, 'I'm just not good enough,' or 'It's a young person's world these days,' or 'They'd never take me seriously.'

Coaching is a wonderful remedy to such problems because it quickly enables people to regain focus. Focus means being free from distractions. We focus most easily on what we find interesting. If you have ever watched a cat play with a mouse or an insect, or a child play with a toy that they find fascinating, you will know that this is true.

Some people confuse focus with effort but these are not the same things. In fact, if we try too hard, we tend to get uptight and tired. We begin to develop a fear of failure and our endeavours become frustrating.

We can develop a quality of focus by noticing what we notice. If, for example, I am coached and discover that I tend to lose eye contact with an audience when giving a presentation, then I should try to note how often it happens next time. The likelihood is that it will happen far less, because I will be more focused.

This is very different from someone telling me not to lose eye contact. Such well-meaning advice will simply increase pressure and probably produce mistakes in other aspects of my presentation.

Focus is a very tenuous thing and we can be distracted quite easily. This is especially likely when we do not really enjoy something (compare reading a novel with reading a textbook).

 Coaching is effective because it works with what the coachee finds most interesting and promotes ever-deeper levels of focus and, consequently, awareness.

Summary

Today we have seen that to be an effective coach requires certain skills and knowledge, as well as a healthy, positive attitude.

Good coaches concern themselves with helping others to raise their levels of self-awareness and encourage them to make positive choices and to take action. They build trust by coaching with an open mind and with great sincerity.

We need to develop and practise the skills of asking probing questions and actively listening. The ultimate aim of coaching is to provide an environment in which the people we coach can immerse themselves in high-quality thinking. Everything we do as human beings is preceded by thought. It follows that the quality of our actions and decisions is tied to the quality of our thinking. This is where coaching can have its most profound effect.

Finally, we saw that coaching provides direction for our thoughts and enables us to focus. Through focus we can make lasting changes and improvements, without the need for someone else to suggest that we do so.

Tomorrow we shall look at a framework for putting all of this into place and at navigating through a coaching session.

SUNDAY
MONDAY
TUESDAY
WEDNESDAY
THURSDAY
FRIDAY
SATURDAY

Fact-check [answers at the back]

1. In helping our coachees restore focus, what should we invite them to do?
   a) Have lunch with us ❏
   b) Notice what they notice ❏
   c) Do as we tell them ❏
   d) Attend a training course ❏

2. What is the purpose of a coach asking questions?
   a) So that the coachee will answer them ❏
   b) To give the coachee cause to think deeply ❏
   c) To impress the coachee by their use of language ❏
   d) To get the coachee to guess what the coach really wants them to do ❏

3. Which of the following is *not* a limiting belief?
   a) I'm too old ❏
   b) I'm not qualified ❏
   c) Anything is possible ❏
   d) I don't deserve it ❏

4. What are the three areas that make up an effective coach?
   a) Qualifications, CV and professional memberships ❏
   b) Attitude, skills and knowledge ❏
   c) Height, weight and age ❏
   d) LinkedIn profile, reputation and status ❏

5. How is a gap in a person's *knowledge* best filled?
   a) By coaching ❏
   b) By instruction ❏
   c) By force ❏
   d) By active listening ❏

6. Why is raising awareness, using questions, useful in coaching?
   a) It saves the coach from doing the work ❏
   b) It demonstrates how clever the coach is ❏
   c) It gets the coachee to think and really notice what is going on ❏
   d) It makes the coaching session last a bit longer ❏

7. What is the level of listening most conducive to coaching known as?
   a) Action listening ❏
   b) Acting as if listening ❏
   c) Actual listening ❏
   d) Active listening ❏

8. Why is generating responsibility using coaching useful?
   a) It allows us to delegate more work ❏
   b) People grow when they learn how to tackle their own problems ❏
   c) There are more people to blame when things go wrong ❏
   d) We can free ourselves from all the mundane tasks ❏

9. Which of these coaching questions is actually an instruction in disguise?
   a) Wouldn't it be better if you took interview notes? ❏
   b) How would you rate your note taking? ❏
   c) What is the effect of note taking on the interviewee? ❏
   d) What are you most aware of when taking notes? ❏

10. Why is building trust through coaching useful?

a) Coachees are more likely to share juicy gossip ❏

b) Coachees will open up and give deeper, more honest answers ❏

c) Coachees will become more loyal to us ❏

d) There's less need to worry that we're using 'textbook' coaching ❏

WEDNESDAY

The coaching ARROW, part 1

Yesterday we explored the various qualities that good coaches develop. Coaching is a particularly powerful development tool because it works on attitude of mind as well as on knowledge and skills.

What we need now is a way of bringing all this together in a framework that is easy to work with and to remember. Here we are going to use a framework known as the coaching ARROW. However, the framework is only a guide; the key principles of raising awareness, generating responsibility and building trust are what are most important.

There are many coaching frameworks around, and you might like to explore some of them after reading this book. The coaching ARROW provides a simple framework around which to construct our coaching questions. Over the next two days we will carefully examine each part of the model so that you will know how to use it to best effect.

Today we introduce the coaching ARROW framework and look at its first two parts:

- Aims
- Reality.

Introduction to the coaching ARROW

Consider the following conversation:

Wife   What shall we do about a holiday this year? I fancy some time in the sun.

Husband   Yes, I agree, and preferably soon.

Wife   Well, I could get a few weeks off in September.

Husband   I can get time off when I like, but I think we'll need to save up.

Wife   We should be able to save enough by September.

Husband   You're right. I'll find out how much we have got saved at the moment.

Wife   I reckon we can have a fortnight in Florida or three weeks in Spain.

Husband   Great, we'll go to Florida for a fortnight in September. Let's both book the time off work tomorrow and I'll call into the travel agent on the way home.

You may not have recognized much coaching going on, but that was exactly what this couple was doing. To begin with, they thought about what they were trying to achieve – they established their **Aims.** Then they thought about how the situation stood at that moment – they considered the **Reality.** There was then some **Reflection** on the gap between the aims and the reality. Next they pondered the **Options** they had and finally they committed to a course of action – the **Way forward.**

Whether they realized it or not, they were using the **coaching ARROW.**

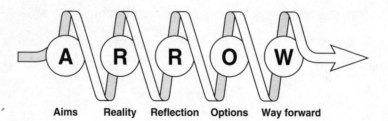

Aims   Reality   Reflection   Options   Way forward

We know that we can develop individuals by raising awareness and generating responsibility in an environment of trust. We can achieve this by asking questions. But what sort of questions should we ask, and in what order? How do such questions promote focus? And how can we guide people towards a positive outcome in a coaching session?

We shall see how the coaching ARROW provides a framework for the coach to ask questions that raise awareness, generate responsibility and build trust. Let us look at the first two parts of the coaching ARROW in detail.

Aims

We all have a variety of aims in every aspect of our lives. We might aim to be effective parents or good managers, or we might aim to lose weight or achieve a certain level of income.

One of the most important things we can do as a coach is help people make sense of their aims and encourage them to commit to a course of action that will help them achieve these aims.

First, we need to appreciate that there are different types of aims. Some aims are quite vague and others are very precise; some aims are more useful to focus on than others.

We can take the example of Olympic athletes. They will probably **dream** of an Olympic gold medal, but it would be dangerous to focus too heavily on this because, no matter how good an athlete they may be, they cannot legislate for what the competition might do.

Instead, athletes tend to set **performance goals**, such as 'personal bests'. In this way they focus on the goals over which they have some control, such as running a race in a certain time or achieving a certain height or distance in a jumping or throwing event.

However, day by day it is most likely that athletes will concentrate on **processes**. For our athlete this might mean working on technique or building stamina. In other words, they focus on the detailed steps necessary to achieve the performance goal that will, in turn, give them the best possible chance of achieving their dream.

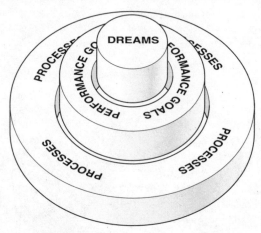

The same is true in business. We might dream of being the top-performing salesperson in the company this year, but we cannot control how the other sales people will perform. We may set a performance goal of achieving five per cent commission income this year, in the hope that such a performance will be good enough to achieve our dream. However, the only way to achieve our performance goals is to concentrate on the processes – for example, our questioning technique and how we handle objections. We might set an aim of asking twice as many 'open' questions as 'closed' ones, or responding to an objection twice before admitting defeat.

The beauty of the coaching ARROW is that it enables the people we coach to think initially about how they would like a situation to change (dreams) and then to devise a specific plan of action to bring it about (processes).

In summary, whenever we think about our aims in life we need:

- **dreams** to provide the inspiration
- **performance goals** to provide the specification
- **processes** to provide the mechanism for achievement.

We shall now look at each of these aspects in more detail.

Dreams

As coaches, one of the most valuable things we can do for people is to encourage them to dream and to think big. Remember that coaches believe in the vast reserves of potential in all people and, because we begin our coaching conversations by discussing aims, it is vital that we encourage people to stretch themselves. At no point must we ever pour scorn on people's high aims and dreams.

More often than not, the thing that holds people back is a set of limiting beliefs, and these beliefs have a habit of becoming true. If, for example, our parents continually winced every time we sang a tune as a small child, then we are likely to believe that we cannot sing. Therefore, we will never be inclined to learn and make changes in order to be able to sing. Vocalists pass air over their vocal cords to make a noise. There is no reason why any of us should not be able to do this and to sing well, given time, support and practice.

Holding positive beliefs and challenging limiting beliefs can bring about incredible performance breakthroughs. Within months of Roger Bannister breaking the four-minute-mile barrier in 1954, a host of other athletes achieved the same feat – they now believed it could be done.

TIP

> *As coaches, we can be our team's advocate and constantly encourage, support and help people to believe that they can achieve their aims.*

Performance goals

In a business setting, we will need to concentrate mainly on performance goals. These will usually come to us through our organization's performance management system. They will include the various standards and targets we are expected to achieve in the coming year or so.

We need to think about making sure that a performance goal is formulated in a way that gives us the best chance of success. We can use coaching questions to make sure that people have constructed well-thought-out and balanced performance goals.

Most people know the mnemonic SMART, and the following table shows a variation on that theme – MACSPROUT.

M	Measurable	How will we know if we have got there?
A	Achievable	Is it within reach?
C	Challenging	Are we motivated to achieve it?
S	Specific	Do we know exactly what is required?
P	Positive	Is it about what is desired or what is to be avoided?
R	Relevant	Will our goal contribute to a bigger picture?
O	Observable	Can we demonstrate our success?
U	Understandable	Is the goal described in clear, simple terms?
T	Time bound	By when will it be achieved?

Processes

Processes are the building blocks that lead to the achievement of performance goals. They are an effective way of helping us focus on the small steps that, in turn, will lead to the big results.

We are concerned with using our coaching skills to help others make changes and to improve their performance. We cannot do this by asking them to change dreams; we cannot even do it by tightening up their performance goals. Change, and therefore improvement, can take place only at the level of process.

We might dream of becoming the World Snooker Champion and set ourselves performance goals on how many tournaments to enter, frames to win, points to score, and so forth. However, in the end it boils down simply to how well we deliver the cue and strike a white ball – this is the only thing we can affect.

Here are some example questions that you might use at this stage in your coaching sessions:

Aims

- What are you trying to achieve in the long term?
- How much personal influence do you have over that?
- What do you want from this discussion?
- What first step could you take?
- Is that challenging yet achievable?
- How will you know if you have succeeded?
- What time frame is involved?

We are now going to look in on a coaching session between Chris and Sam. Chris is the Team Leader in the Customer Service section and provides coaching to Sam who, it appears, has some time management problems.

Chris OK, Sam, how would you like your time management to be, eventually?

Sam I just want to be one of those people who always seems to be in control, who can find things when they need them and take on extra work when needs be.

Chris Is that within your power, Sam?

Sam Well, I don't see why not. Some people do dump on me, but then I suppose it's up to me to be a bit more assertive. Yes, I think it is down to me.

Chris What would you like to achieve today?

Sam The thing I'm most concerned about is my habit of putting things off. I tell myself that, if I can clear this and that out of the way, I'll be able to concentrate on my big projects. The problem is the day just becomes full of more this and thats.

Chris What's the first step in solving this?

Sam I want to get my current project finished by the end of the week, no matter what the distractions.

Chris Can you do that?

Sam We'll have to see, but I'd like to.

Chris How will you judge your success?

Sam Obviously, if I get the project finished, I'll know I was successful. But, more importantly, if I've been able to avoid putting it off, then hopefully I'll be developing better habits.

We can see that these questions have enabled Sam not only to think about what she wants in the long term but also to focus on one thing she can work on straight away. Chris may or may not agree that putting things off is the major issue but, in the true spirit of coaching, he has recognized that his view does not matter.

The coaching ARROW enables us to help others to formulate and understand these three types of aims. We can then use it to help people understand the current reality of their situation, the processes they are currently employing and which ones they might need to change.

Reality

If the aims uncovered in a coaching session represent a destination – where a person is trying to get to – it follows that we also need to think about the starting point. Part of our role as coach is to help people understand the reality of their situation.

Perception and interpretation

The most important thing to recognize as we coach people through this stage is that what we call reality is all a matter of perception.

We all constantly interpret our environment according to our own experiences. As a result, we construct our own unique model of the world, which serves to guide us through life. We do not have to deal with every interaction we have as if it were a new experience. Our model of the world gives us patterns to recognize familiar objects or events. Having seen a tree in our own country, we can recognize the same thing if we encounter one in, say, Australia.

However, not everyone will interpret the same thing in the same way. I might ask you, for example, whether this shape is concave or convex:

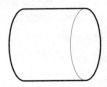

Of course, there is no right answer; it is all a matter of perspective. Some people will see the shape as convex, others as concave.

What has all this to do with coaching? The important perspective in coaching is that of the person being coached: it is their version of reality that counts.

Case study

John was a salesperson who sought some coaching on how he might better answer customer objections during the sales conversation. He approached Mary for some coaching on this and, having discussed his aims, they began to explore the reality of John's situation. John was concerned about this aspect of his sales technique and rated himself as one of the poorest in the team in this regard.

Mary disagreed. She insisted that John was one of her best performers as far as handling objections was concerned, and she suggested that John should think of another performance area on which to be coached. John thanked Mary for the encouragement but explained once more that this was his number-one issue at the moment and it was affecting his performance overall. He instinctively knew that, if he could get over these feelings, his performance would really soar.

Mary became so irritated with John for failing to see what she saw as the reality of the situation that she ended the coaching session and suggested that John might like to return when he had something sensible to discuss. She had failed to help John raise his self-awareness, she had reclaimed the responsibility for John's learning and she had shattered the relationship of trust.

Needless to say, John did not seek her coaching again.

It is dangerous to impose our view of reality on to the other person. We need to be alive to the possibility of different perceptions and perspectives.

How many squares can you see in this picture?

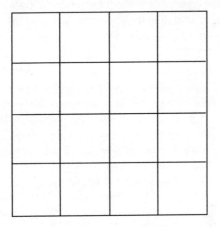

The correct answer is 30:

- 1 whole square
- 16 individual squares
- 9 squares of 4 units
- 4 squares of 9 units.

Look again until you can see all 30. This gives us another important lesson when we are thinking about reality, namely that the true picture of reality often only emerges after we have looked several times. It is worthwhile spending some time in a coaching session on the Reality stage.

We should welcome the fact that the people we coach may see things differently from us. It creates a sense of diversity and can throw up all sorts of new ways of taking a situation forward that would never be uncovered if we all thought in the same way.

Encouraging a positive outlook

Coaching is a powerful tool for improving performance in any area. In an organizational setting we should never use it just as a means of addressing poor performance. Sometimes even the best-performing team members are still operating below the level of their potential. They, too, deserve to benefit from coaching and to see how they might improve.

Coaching is also a valuable tool for problem solving and dealing with difficult issues. Most coaching at work is used for this purpose.

When we are coaching someone through the Reality stage, it is possible that they may get quite disheartened when they realize how big a task or challenge they face. It may be necessary to encourage them to think through all the things that are going well in a situation – there will always be some! – to help them see a balanced picture.

This is not the same as imposing our view; it is simply encouraging the other person to recognize that an accurate view of reality includes acknowledging what is going well. More importantly, it sets a positive tone for discussing solutions later in the coaching session.

Here are some examples of the sorts of questions we can ask at this stage:

Reality

- What's happening now?
- How much/How often is that happening?
- How does this make you feel?
- Who else is involved?
- What happens to them?
- What have you tried so far?
- What results did you get?

We shall now look at how this works out for Chris and Sam:

Chris Tell me about how things are now.
Sam What, generally?
Chris Tell me about the project you're working on this week.
Sam OK, it's to do with collating statistics on how quickly we respond to complaints. It's really detailed work and I need to concentrate, so I say to myself to get

	everything else out of the way before lunch and then concentrate on the project in the afternoon.
Chris	Does that work out?
Sam	No, not really. There's usually something that comes up to attend to in the afternoon.
Chris	How does this make you feel?
Sam	I get annoyed. I know that the stuff I do in the morning isn't really important. I've just wasted time when I know I could really have worked on the project.
Chris	Is anyone else affected by this?
Sam	Actually, yes. Denise needs the statistics by the start of next week or her own work will be delayed. I'd hate to let her down.
Chris	How have you tried to solve this problem before?
Sam	For a while I disciplined myself to do my important work in the morning when I felt fresh, and then have a nice afternoon doing odd bits and pieces. But after a while I just slipped back into my old habits.

Sam is becoming highly aware of the situation and is beginning to see things more clearly. Chris has used the coaching questions carefully to go with the flow of Sam's answers. They are now ready to reflect on what they have learned by considering the gap between aims and reality.

Summary

Today has been about exploring the first two parts of the coaching ARROW.

We saw that people will have a variety of aims and that one of our roles as a coach is to help them make sense of them and to separate them out into *dreams*, *performance goals* and *processes*. These three types of aims are connected: if we help people to identify changes in the processes they use, they have a greater chance of achieving their performance goals (provided these goals have been carefully constructed) and, in turn, of realizing their dreams.

We went on to look at coaching questions based around reality. It is vital when we are coaching that we act as the casual observer and resist the temptation to voice our own views and opinions.

The Reality stage is especially important as it deals in the hard facts of what is actually happening. A huge amount of useful learning takes place when people are truly able to focus on the here and now.

Tomorrow we shall look at the rest of the coaching ARROW.

Fact-check [answers at the back]

1. What does the A in the coaching ARROW stand for?
a) Achievements ❏
b) Aims ❏
c) Aspirations ❏
d) Armchair ❏

2. Why is setting sound performance goals an important part of coaching around aims?
a) Performance goals provide inspiration ❏
b) Performance goals provide a specification of success ❏
c) Performance goals provide a mechanism for achievement ❏
d) Performance goals keep management happy ❏

3. Which of these criteria is *not* a quality of an effective performance goal?
a) Challenging ❏
b) Relevant ❏
c) Achievable ❏
d) Passionate ❏

4. Which of the following is the only way to achieve our performance goals?
a) Focus on processes ❏
b) Daydream ❏
c) Rely on help from others ❏
d) Work really hard and hope for the best ❏

5. Which of these statements is *true* for a coach?
a) At no point must we ever pour scorn on people's high aims and dreams ❏
b) There's no point in dreaming; it means you're asleep ❏
c) People need to learn to be more realistic ❏
d) Never risk failing and making a fool of yourself ❏

6. What does the first R in the coaching ARROW stand for?
a) Reasons ❏
b) Rationale ❏
c) Ratatouille ❏
d) Reality ❏

7. What should we do when we and our coachees have a different view of reality?
a) Talk it through until they agree that we're right ❏
b) Take an interest in how they came to their point of view ❏
c) Challenge them to prove that they're right ❏
d) Ignore the point and press on ❏

8. Which of these statements is true of the reality stage?
a) The current situation cannot change, so there is no point discussing it ❏
b) There is only ever one correct way of viewing a situation ❏
c) A moment or two thinking about reality is more than enough ❏
d) The true picture of reality often takes time to emerge ❏

9. An accurate view of reality...
a) Means accepting that others are right and we are wrong ❏
b) Needs little time to get right ❏
c) Includes acknowledging what's going well ❏
d) Comes when we smile our way past even the trickiest problems ❏

10. What does establishing the aims and reality enable us to do?
a) Clarify what our coachees aspire to and from where they start ❏
b) Set targets for our coachees ❏
c) Finish coaching quickly if we're pushed for time ❏
d) Report back on any problems identified ❏

THURSDAY

The coaching ARROW, part 2

We have seen that coaching is a way of nurturing talent and helping people to perform their best work, the potential for which is already there. We have uncovered the idea that, in organizations, managers are ideally placed to provide coaching to their staff, but that doing so requires a significant shift in our approach to communication. We need to do much less telling and much more asking and listening. We need to organize our questions using a logical progression, and one means of doing this is with the coaching ARROW.

The first two parts of the coaching ARROW, Aims and Reality, serve to promote the highest levels of self-awareness in the people we coach. We have already discovered that being self-aware provides us with more choices about the changes we can make to improve our performance.

This type of reflective thinking has its place in the coaching conversation, too, where it is important to take stock, to conclude and reconsider lest we move too quickly into plans and actions that are premature.

Today we will look at the remaining three parts of the model:

- Reflection
- Options
- Way forward.

Reflection

The Reflection part of the coaching ARROW provides the person being coached with an opportunity to consider what has been discovered so far. Depending on the underlying issue and how much time is available for coaching in one session, reflection may prove to be a major or minor part of the whole process.

True enlightenment often happens in this part of the coaching process; this is what some have described as 'aha!' moments.

Time can be a useful tool here. Some coaches have had great success in stopping a coaching session after Aims and Reality and giving the person being coached the Reflection questions to think about before they meet up again to explore Options and Way forward.

Remember that the coaching ARROW is merely a framework for coaching, and the model must be used flexibly. It is not possible for us to coach effectively by simply reeling off a series of questions. The needs and agenda of the person being coached must take priority at all times.

We must use the Reflection stage particularly carefully because the person being coached may have already reflected subconsciously when they have answered the questions under Aims and Reality.

Similarly, it is worth encouraging the people we coach to reflect continuously throughout the session and, if necessary, to refine their aims or review the reality of the situation.

These are the sorts of questions we could ask at the Reflection stage:

Reflection

- How big is the gap between aims and reality?
- How realistic are your aims?
- How certain are you about the reality of the situation?
- How could you find out more?
- What assumptions are you making?
- Have you been totally honest with yourself?
- What's really going on?

Back to Chris and Sam:

Chris   OK, Sam, we've explored where you are trying to get to and where you are starting from. How big a gap is there?

Sam   Thinking about it, I'm quite a long way from being this person in control that I described. I need to deal with the problem of putting things off first.

Chris   So are your aims realistic?

Sam   My short-term aim to stop putting things off is realistic, but I need to think more thoroughly about time management generally.

Chris   Well, we can certainly look at that another time, but how certain are you of the reality of your situation?

Sam   Well, I feel certain I know how things affect me, but I do need to find out more about the knock-on effect with others.

Chris   How will you find out?

Sam   Oh, that's easy – I'll just ask them.

Chris   Have you been totally honest with yourself?

Sam   Yes, I think so.

Chris   What's really going on, Sam?

Sam   To be honest, I find some of these projects a bit overwhelming. There's usually a need for a lot of figure work, which isn't really my strength, and I guess I just put these things off because I know I won't enjoy the work and I'll struggle.

In this case the Reflection questions have been very useful because they have taken Sam to a greater level of self-awareness, and the true nature of the coaching issue has now emerged.

Options

The coaching questions we ask under the first three headings of the coaching ARROW help the people we coach to decide where it is they want to go, where exactly they are starting from and how big the gap is between the two points.

We now need to help them think through the various options they have in dealing with their issues and moving towards their aims.

The greatest pitfall here is for the person being coached to grasp the first idea that comes to mind. It may be that this proves to be absolutely appropriate, but the good coach will encourage their people to be highly imaginative and creative in considering options and to be constantly alert for new insights.

'Stuck' thinking

Most days I walk into my office through the front door and take the same route to my desk. I have done this for years and it can be evidenced by the carpet between these two points being markedly worn. Imagine if I was being coached on how I might arrive at my desk more alert and stimulated for the day's work. It would be very difficult for me to think of any alternative to my tried-and-tested route of the straight line from the door to the desk. In fact, if anyone suggested a different route to me, I would be likely to say, 'It would take too long,' or 'It's a waste of time,' or 'I've never done it that way before,' or 'That's just not how it's done here.' All of which may or may not be true.

However, if my coach encouraged me to think creatively, I might consider walking around the edge of the office, past the window. As I thought about it, I might realize that this would give me an opportunity to look at the river, which I always find stimulating. In other words, I would have hit upon a novel approach to achieving my aim.

Similarly, because I am enjoying the coaching session and I feel free to allow my thinking to run a little wild, I might think about moving from the door to my desk in a figure of eight. As I thought about that option, I might realize that this would take me right past the table where I keep the books and articles I keep meaning to read but that I keep forgetting about. I would pass the kettle, which I could switch on as I went and, finally, I would go past the computer printer that I do not normally pass but that I end up having to switch on later in the day.

In this way I have developed fresh insights and found new benefits, just by 'unsticking' my existing thinking.

 New thinking almost always leads to new benefits.

Case study

In the early 1970s Art Fry, a technician at 3M, wanted a bookmark that would neither fall out nor damage his book. He knew that a colleague, Dr Spencer, had developed a type of glue that could stick to most surfaces but that left nothing behind after removal. Art applied a little of this glue to a piece of paper, and the Post-it® note was born.

Breaking assumptions

In a similar way, people labour under certain assumptions about what is actually possible within situations at work. We tell ourselves that 'There isn't enough time,' or 'We haven't got the budget,' or 'I don't have the authority.'

Again, these thoughts may or may not be true, but it is very useful in a coaching session to free people of these constraints to see what other options might become available. So we might ask, 'What if you had more time, what could you do?' or 'What if you had more money...?', and so on.

Of course, we cannot pretend that there are no barriers or restrictions, but what we are really trying to discover, through coaching, is whether these barriers are genuine or just assumptions. It is even possible that a restriction that was there some time ago may no longer exist – we just assume that it does.

Case study

A distribution manager wanted to reorganize the routes that his company used to supply dairy products to a number of grocery stores in their region.

He was told that his new routes would not work because the stores farthest out wanted their deliveries on a Monday and would not accept any other day. However, the distribution manager spoke to the storekeepers and discovered that, although they wanted a fast, reliable service, they were not concerned about which day of the week their deliveries took place.

Some time later, at a social event, a retired delivery person explained that the reason deliveries to the outermost stores had always been made on a Monday was historical and was because the horses were fresh after their Sunday rest!

These are some example questions that you might use at the Options stage in your coaching sessions:

Options

- What could you do about all this?
- What else could you try?
- What if you had more...?
- Whose advice could you seek?
- What suggestions would they have?
- What would you do if you knew you couldn't fail?
- Would you like another suggestion?

Let us see how Chris and Sam get on with this part of the coaching ARROW:

Chris What could you do about all this, Sam?

Sam Well, I know I said it hadn't worked before but I could try doing my project work in the mornings again.

Chris What else could you try?

Sam I'm not sure. Perhaps I could learn more about spreadsheets to make the figure work easier.

Chris What would you do if you were the boss?

Sam If I were Denise, I'd have put everyone on the spreadsheet course. If we all knew how to use them, I'm sure we'd get these projects done in half the time and then they wouldn't seem so daunting.

Chris That sounds like an interesting idea. Would you like another suggestion, too?

Sam Not at the moment, thanks. I've come up with a couple of ideas now so I think I'd like to see how they work out.

Sam has moved away from her 'stuck' thinking about rearranging her day. She has begun to explore solutions to the underlying issue of being worried by the amount of figure work involved in the project. Some coaches may have gone with her first suggestion of rearranging her day, particularly if *they* felt that was the best idea.

Notice that Chris probably has one or two suggestions based on his own experience that he thinks Sam may find helpful. However, rather than just offer his advice, he asks Sam if she would like to hear his suggestion. In this way he has kept Sam responsible for her own learning and not upset the trust that they have established.

 More often than not, the people you coach will be only too delighted to hear any suggestions that you may have, but be careful to do this in the true spirit of coaching.

Way forward

'Pray for potatoes, but pick up a hoe.'

Anon.

Despite all the energy that we have put into navigating the first four stages of the coaching ARROW, so far we have accomplished very little. In truth we have thought, pondered, intellectualized and navel-gazed, but changed nothing. This is why the final part of the model, Way forward, is so vital. This is where we turn thought into action.

If we have coached well to this point, we should begin to see the energy levels of the people we coach rise. They will realize that they are resourceful and that they can move their own issues forward, and they will become excited at the prospect of doing so. It can be really useful if we, as coaches, mirror this excitement to signal our belief in them and to encourage a definite course of meaningful action.

Many coaches report that this part of the process is largely automatic, and it is often simply a matter of making sure that people plan their actions in a sensible and logical way.

Here are some example questions that we might use at this stage during our coaching sessions:

Way forward

- So, what exactly are you going to do?
- When are you going to do it?
- Who needs to know?
- How and when will you tell them?
- What resources do you need?
- How will you get them?
- Will this take you towards your aims?
- What do you need me to do?
- What is your commitment to this course of action on a scale of 1–10?

We are now asking 'What *will* you do?' rather than 'What *can* you do?' We should check that the course of action decided upon will deliver the aims established at the start of the session, and we should offer any assistance that we can provide.

The final question is interesting because it asks the person being coached to rate their commitment to taking the course of action that they have thought out. We might think that, having gone through the model thoroughly and carefully, the answer here will always be 10, but this is not necessarily so. Sometimes a person will be reluctant to move forward, despite a well-constructed coaching session. When this happens, it is usually because of a barrier somewhere.

Perhaps it is because the person believes that other parties involved in the issue will not play their part in moving things forward. Sometimes it is because people are absolutely clear about what needs doing and certain that it will work, but they lack the courage to put the plan into action.

Generally speaking, if we get an answer to the final question of anything less than 7, the chances are that the person will not take action and our coaching session will have proven ineffective.

We need to discover what the barrier is by asking a further question: 'What would make it a 10?' In answering this question, the person being coached will come to understand what is preventing full commitment and we will perhaps have uncovered a more deep-rooted coaching issue.

Sometimes, when we get to Way forward, we find that the person has articulated the same solution two or three times in the session. This is perfectly OK and suggests that the solution is one to which the person will be most committed. Working through the coaching ARROW is rather like going up a spiral staircase. We will see the same things each time we go round but always from a slightly new perspective, and we build a more complete picture. Therefore we can now see how Chris and Sam get on with this final part.

Chris	OK, Sam. What are you going to do?
Sam	I'm going to approach Denise and ask to go to the training room to work through the online training package on spreadsheets.
Chris	When will you do that?
Sam	I'll see Denise this afternoon and I want to do the training tomorrow.
Chris	Will this take you towards your aims?
Sam	If I can take the time to finally get over this business of being put off by the figure work, I'll easily finish the project by the end of the week. This will be a big step towards feeling in control.
Chris	What's your commitment to taking this action on a scale of 1–10?
Sam	Well, I'd put it at about 6
Chris	What would make it a 10?
Sam	I'm not sure Denise will be happy about me asking for the time to do the training. She can be a tough person to approach.
Chris	What could you do?
Sam	I'm not sure. Perhaps if, rather than just ask for the time, I explained what we'd done here and how it will benefit both of us in the long term, she'd be more willing. Yes, that's it – 10 out of 10 now!
Chris	Is there anything else, Sam?
Sam	No. Thank you very much; you've been really helpful.

Sam is now completely committed to tackling a major part of her time-management problems. She is fully aware of her strengths and weaknesses in this area and has taken responsibility for moving the issue forward. As she puts her plan into action, she may encounter unforeseen problems, but with her renewed motivation and energy she is likely to deal with them and keep moving forward. At the very least, her coaching session with Chris will have helped her to realize that she is a resourceful person who can tackle her own problems.

For his part, Chris has acted as an ideal coach for Sam because he has encouraged her to think through her issues for herself. Arguably, he has not forced her to come up with a solution that she was not aware of at some level anyway. However, he has enabled her finally to take action and to stop it being something she will 'get around to one day'.

There is much more to the art of coaching than just firing off a series of questions. Listening, really listening, to the answers you are given is probably twice as important.

Summary

Today we finished developing our understanding of the questioning sequence known as the coaching ARROW.

In our discussion of the Reflection stage, we considered the questions designed to promote reflection, and saw how these can provide a more solid platform to take a coaching session forward. They add clarity to the thinking that takes place during the Aims and Reality stages. We went on to look at the Options stage and saw how useful it can be to allow people to be almost self-indulgent with their thinking. Finally, we considered how we encourage people to turn thought into action by working through the questions under Way forward.

A word of caution may be useful at this stage. The coaching ARROW, or any other coaching question sequence, is merely that: a series of questions designed to take a conversation from start to finish. Knowing which questions *not* to ask is a vital skill, and a good coach will use silence and pauses as an effective way of promoting deep thought. Without an appreciation of the underlying principles of awareness, responsibility and trust, coaching questions are useless.

Now that we have a detailed understanding of the mechanics of coaching, we need to turn our sights to putting coaching into context.

SUNDAY MONDAY TUESDAY WEDNESDAY THURSDAY FRIDAY SATURDAY

Fact-check [answers at the back]

1. What is the coaching ARROW?
   a) A coaching model ❏
   b) A questioning sequence ❏
   c) All we need to be an effective coach ❏
   d) A substitute for having to think about our own questions ❏

2. Why is going through the coaching ARROW like climbing a spiral staircase?
   a) We may see the same things, but from different angles ❏
   b) Working here is like going round in circles ❏
   c) Coaching can be exhausting ❏
   d) When you've reached the top the only way is down ❏

3. What does the second R in the coaching ARROW stand for?
   a) Reality ❏
   b) Reflection ❏
   c) Raison d'être ❏
   d) Ravioli ❏

4. Which of these statements is true of the Reflection stage?
   a) It is only appropriate between Reality and Options ❏
   b) It can be missed completely if we need to rush ❏
   c) It is useful throughout the coaching sequence ❏
   d) It is an opportunity for the coach to give advice ❏

5. What does the O in the coaching ARROW stand for?
   a) Outcomes ❏
   b) Objectives ❏
   c) Objections ❏
   d) Options ❏

6. Which of these statements is *not* an assumption?
   a) There's no money ❏
   b) Management won't sign that off ❏
   c) We can't afford it ❏
   d) The training budget is £100k ❏

7. What does the W in the coaching ARROW stand for?
   a) Way behind ❏
   b) Way to go! ❏
   c) Way forward ❏
   d) Woe is me! ❏

8. What is the Way forward stage about?
   a) Turning thoughts into action ❏
   b) Project inception plans ❏
   c) Management briefings ❏
   d) More thoughts ❏

9. When coachees give a low score to the commitment question, what does it indicate?
   a) Our coaching has been a resounding success ❏
   b) Our coaching has been an unmitigated disaster ❏
   c) There remains a barrier somewhere ❏
   d) The coachee hasn't really been trying ❏

10. What gives a good indication of successful coaching?
   a) Rising energy levels ❏
   b) A very tired coachee ❏
   c) Running out of questions to ask ❏
   d) Lots of paperwork ❏

Coaching
in context

We have now covered the underlying principles and processes of coaching and have developed our understanding to the point where we are able to undertake high-quality, person-centred coaching sessions with individuals and groups.

One way of using coaching is as a distinct task. This means a series of organized coaching sessions that take place at an agreed time and schedule, usually in a private meeting room or similar. We would expect to see such sessions followed up with notes and action plans, which both coach and coachee sign as a record of what has been agreed.

Alternatively, we can use coaching in a much less formal and structured way. Given an understanding of the principles and questions, there is no reason why coaching cannot form part of most natural day-to-day conversations at work.

We must remember, however, that coaching does not take place in a vacuum. We need to recognize some of the other factors that happen at work, so that good coaching becomes a useful and practical tool rather than an academic exercise.

In this chapter we shall consider the following areas:

- the limitations of the coaching ARROW
- cultural differences
- when to coach
- following up
- the reluctant coachee
- coaching applications
- myths revisited.

The limitations of the coaching ARROW

Like any model or mnemonic, the coaching ARROW is only useful if it helps us to remember the underlying principles. It is not meant to suggest that asking questions in sequence is all there is to effective coaching.

Case study

Ravi worked as a Client Relationship Manager for a hotel and conference centre. He was not comfortable with his ability to handle requests for discounts from regular clients. And so he asked Sue, his manager, for some coaching on his negotiation skills.

Sue wanted to be helpful and so she listed the coaching ARROW questions on a piece of paper, with space underneath to record Ravi's answers.

Sue and Ravi moved to a quiet area, and Sue carefully asked the questions in sequence and took detailed notes of Ravi's answers. Ravi noticed that Sue looked down at her notes after she had asked each question, and did not make eye contact with him or make any kind of verbal or non-verbal response to his answers. He found that this made it difficult to focus and think deeply. He was not convinced that Sue was really trying to help, but instead was working through the coaching session quite mechanically in an effort to get it done and out of the way.

He also noticed that many of Sue's questions started with words like 'Don't you think you ought...?' and 'Wouldn't it be better if...?'. This made him think that Sue was just trying to steer him towards her own ideas.

Later that day, a colleague asked Ravi how the session had gone, and he replied that it had been a complete waste of time.

We can see that, without a deep understanding of the underlying principles of awareness, responsibility and trust, we might do more harm than good in a coaching session. On the other hand, when we do understand the underlying principles, it is possible to ask coaching questions in a much more natural and conversational way. This also enables us to concentrate more on the person being coached, than on trying to remember what question comes next.

Cultural differences

When we talk about culture and how it affects the coaching relationship, it is not just a matter of considering nationality, race or religion. We also need to take into account the cultures people may have become used to in previous employment, in education or in the home. More importantly, perhaps, we need to think about the prevailing culture in our own organizations if coaching has not been the norm.

There are many dimensions to culture and we need to consider, for example:

● **directness**
Will the coaching approach work every time or will people sometimes prefer some straightforward feedback?

● **hierarchy**
How do we position the coaching relationship in the normal 'pecking order'?

● **consensus**
What have people been used to and how much scope is there to move up and down the communication spectrum described on Monday?

● **individualism**
Do we apply coaching at the level of the team or the individual?

Of course, there are no right or wrong answers to these questions. They are simply views that we need to think about in order to give coaching its most solid platform.

When to coach

I am often asked how long a coaching session should last and how often sessions should take place. This is as impossible to answer as it is to say how long is a piece of string. What we do know is that coaching is an extremely flexible tool and there are a great many ways to use it to good effect.

Typically, coaching is prearranged for a specific date and time. The coach and the individual normally retire to a separate area and conduct the coaching in a fairly formal setting.

Once again, provided that the basic principles of coaching are followed, this can be extremely effective. However, it does not have to be done in this way. Effective coaching can take place when talking over lunch or chatting around the coffee machine or water cooler. It all depends on the preferences of the person being coached, the complexity of the subject and how much time we have available.

Similarly, we need to think about who decides whether coaching is needed at all. We, as managers, might need to instigate coaching because of some organizational change. Alternatively, we might prefer to invite people to seek our coaching when they become aware of an issue they would like to move forward.

The importance of trust

Trust is the key. As long as the people we coach trust that we are doing it for their benefit and that their needs are paramount, they will be honest and open in their responses and participate in the coaching in a meaningful way.

How can people trust the harvest, unless they see it sown?'

Mary Renault, English writer

Following up

We should perhaps consider replacing the coaching ARROW with the coaching ARROWF! The F stands for *Follow-up*.

Case study

Many years ago I had a problem with workload management. I was in the habit of organizing my intray with the easy, straightforward tasks at the top and the more important work at the bottom. Unfortunately, this sometimes meant that I was spending time on the easy tasks at the expense of the more important ones.

I sought coaching on this issue and decided to organize my intray in exactly the same way but to turn it upside down. In effect, I was now working from the bottom upwards.

I tried this for a few days with some success, but I was struggling to break old habits. Unexpectedly, my coach phoned me and asked me how I was getting on. We chatted for a few minutes, and by the end of the conversation I was once more fully committed to my plan. I stuck to my task and I eventually broke the bad habit and began to develop other ways of prioritizing my work.

Without follow-up, the chances of our coaching being successful are reduced. Coaching is normally about aiding people to change behaviours that are proving unhelpful. Unfortunately, these sorts of behaviours do not give up without a fight. The ongoing support of a coach can be the difference between successfully establishing a new pattern and slipping back into old habits.

Like coaching itself, this does not need to be a huge task. A two-minute phone conversation or a three-line email can be enough to let the people we coach know that we are there for them.

TIP *Useful follow-up questions to ask include:*
- *What actually happened?*
- *Is that what you wanted?*
- *What have you learned?*
- *How can you improve on this?*

The reluctant coachee

Some of the coaches I have worked with complain that some people just do not want to be coached. They claim that people give only superficial answers to the coaching questions and they look bored and fed up with the whole thing.

Remember that, as coaches, we have a positive view of people and we believe that it is human nature to want to grow and develop. Therefore, we need to think about what might be going wrong here.

Often, a lack of trust causes a breakdown in the coaching relationship. It might be that people mistrust the organization and think that coaching is just another control mechanism. They might even think that coaching is just another fad and that it will go away if they keep their head down.

In any event, something must have happened at some point to make people feel this way. If we work with people gradually and over the long term, we can use coaching to uncover what it is. Then, and only then, will we have got down to the real coaching issues.

We must also accept that people will not always trust us as coaches. Trust is earned, not given. If we have done things in the past that have generated a sense of mistrust, such feelings will not disappear simply because we have 'found' coaching.

In addition, we must not hide behind coaching or use it for the wrong reasons. If a member of the team is being continually late, for example, then this is a matter for specific feedback and, if necessary, discipline. It cannot be coached out of them. Once there is acceptance of the intrinsic performance issue, then coaching comes into its own as a means of addressing it.

MY COACH IS BIGGER
THAN YOURS

Coaching applications

Coaching can be helpful for several purposes in a variety of situations:

- **one-on-one development**
  We have seen throughout the book that coaching is a powerful tool for individual development because of its person-centred approach.

- **team development**
  Coaching can help the members of teams to shape their strengths and weaknesses and focus their attention on team goals. The coaching ARROW also provides a neat way of organizing the agenda for any team meeting or get-together.

- **motivation**
  One of the reasons coaching works so well is because it appeals to people's internal drivers. It is an enjoyable experience that enables people to learn and to perform better.

- **self-development**
  There is no reason why we cannot work through the coaching ARROW for ourselves, although it is better to have the support of another person.

At the simplest level, coaching is a way of moving things forward and it can be useful in any aspect of life – at or outside work.

Myths revisited

We can now go back to the various statements that on Sunday we thought may or may not have been myths. How do they stand up in light of the things we have learned about coaching?

Everything's fine; we don't really have any problems and so we don't need coaching

Coaching is a marvellous tool for problem solving and, although in most cases people will seek coaching because they have a problem to solve, it would be a mistake to limit it to this purpose alone.

Some managers suffer a sort of 'prodigal son' mentality and spend all their time and energy addressing the poorest performers. Do not assume that people who are performing well do not have vast reserves of potential that might be released through coaching. Even the best performers benefit from coaching. We need only to look at the world of sport to know that this is true.

I'm not a manager or team leader so I don't have anyone to coach

Typically, coaching is delivered by managers to staff or by team leaders to team members, and this is usually because companies and other businesses are organized in a hierarchy. But it does not have to be this way.

Anyone can be a coach. The skills of coaching are not in any way connected to age, status, experience or job role. Similarly, coaching can be delivered in any direction and should not be limited to a top-down approach from team leader to team member. Why not have nurses coaching consultants, printers coaching designers or classroom assistants coaching teachers?

I haven't time to coach

We might respond to this by suggesting that there is not time not to coach! We must, however, recognize that coaching is in many ways an investment that pays back in the medium to long term. It can be very difficult for managers to decide whether to take the time to coach an individual through a problem or whether to deal with the situation themselves. This is a matter of choice and taking responsibility.

Effective managers base their decision on an evaluation of the needs of the situation and the people involved in order to make an informed choice. Less effective managers will tend to think that solving all the team's problems themselves is part of their role, perhaps in the mistaken belief that this is the essence of strong leadership.

Managers who coach, however, are constantly generating responsibility and building trust with the teams and individuals that they manage. They are able to take on a more authoritative style when the need arises, without alienating the team or damaging trust.

I can't coach – I have no expertise in the underlying subject

We need expertise to teach, but not to coach. In coaching, expertise can be quite dangerous. It provides temptation to slip back into telling people what to do, giving advice and 'rescuing' people, rather than letting them learn.

Where we find ourselves coaching people in matters that we do have expertise in, we must work hard to resist this temptation and remember that coaching is about helping people to learn and to become independent and resourceful. This is to everyone's benefit over time.

I went on a course about this, but then it was called 'feedback'. That's all coaching really is

Well-constructed feedback can be extremely valuable to people as they try to improve performance in any area. However, it is limited to what we can observe and notice and this can be of no consequence if the performance issue is to do with how people *feel*.

Poorly constructed feedback can do lasting damage and reinforce limiting beliefs. Coaching avoids these pitfalls by concentrating on the needs and experiences of the person being coached.

This is just a fancy new name for what I've been doing for years – training people!

Training has its place, of course, and when done well it is an excellent way of arming people with the basic skills and knowledge that they need to perform their roles. Coaching comes into its own when we want to develop performance and allow people to utilize the full extent of the knowledge and skills that they have gained through training.

Unlike training, coaching derives its agenda from the needs of the individual, it takes place at work (which is where learning really happens) and it can be delivered at more or less any time and anywhere.

IT'S EITHER LET ME COACH YOU NOW – OR WAIT UNTIL THE COURSE NEXT THURSDAY

Summary

Today has been about looking at coaching in practical terms. We have seen that we need to apply our skills and knowledge of coaching carefully and to recognize other factors that may be going on at the same time. We have seen again that the coaching ARROW is merely a tool for the effective coach and is not, by itself, all there is to coaching.

We explored the cultural dimension and recognized that all people at work are a combination of a number of influences that can affect their response to coaching.

Knowing when to coach is part of the skill and art of effective coaching. Coaching when it is inappropriate to do so can do more harm than good. We have also seen how the effective coach will make sure that agreed actions are followed up and use a range of sensitive tactics to deal with reluctant coachees.

Finally, we reviewed some of the comments we first encountered on Sunday and exposed them for the myths they are.

Tomorrow we will conclude our week's study by looking at how coaching can play a vital role in the wider organization.

SUNDAY

MONDAY

TUESDAY

WEDNESDAY

THURSDAY

FRIDAY

SATURDAY

Fact-check [answers at the back]

1. Why is it necessary to consider the prevailing culture before introducing coaching?
   a) You get into trouble these days if you don't ❑
   b) We might inadvertently say something offensive ❑
   c) It will give coaching its most solid platform ❑
   d) It provides a defence against any claims of bias ❑

2. Which of the following is *not* a dimension of culture?
   a) Directness ❑
   b) Hierarchy ❑
   c) Individualism ❑
   d) Age ❑

3. If we added an F to the coaching ARROW, what would it stand for?
   a) Fatigue ❑
   b) Failure ❑
   c) Follow-up ❑
   d) Final analysis ❑

4. What does the ideal coaching session need to do?
   a) Last about 90 minutes ❑
   b) Take place in a separate room ❑
   c) Result in a formal, written action plan ❑
   d) Be determined by the needs of the coachee and the situation ❑

5. What characterizes the unhelpful behaviour that coaching aims to help change?
   a) It is inevitable ❑
   b) It is unchangeable ❑
   c) It does not give up without a fight ❑
   d) It requires deep psychoanalysis to change ❑

6. Which of these is *not* a useful follow-up coaching question?
   a) What actually happened? ❑
   b) Why did you let that happen? ❑
   c) What have you learned? ❑
   d) How can you improve? ❑

7. Which of these is *not* a coaching application?
   a) One-to-one development ❑
   b) Team development ❑
   c) Gross misconduct ❑
   d) Improving motivation ❑

8. What may cause a breakdown in a coaching relationship?
   a) A lack of meeting room space ❑
   b) A lack of trust ❑
   c) A cynical coachee ❑
   d) An inexperienced coach ❑

9. Why is feedback of only limited use in coaching?
   a) You cannot give people feedback on how they *felt* ❑
   b) It takes up too much time ❑
   c) You would have to be the coachee's boss ❑
   d) It requires formal, written evidence ❑

10. Coaching is a relatively new field, and so...
    a) We can make it up as we go along ❑
    b) It is inevitable that some myths have arisen ❑
    c) It should be left to the academics ❑
    d) It is too soon to use it in a work situation ❑

SATURDAY

Coaching in organizations

Over the last six days we have explored the nature of coaching. We have looked in depth at the skills and techniques involved in becoming a useful and effective coach for the individuals and teams with whom we work.

The world of work today is tough: it is fast paced, pressurized, complex and constantly changing. Coaching is an especially powerful tool for the modern leader or manager, because it is a highly effective way of developing individual and consequently organizational performance. While anecdotal evidence suggests that coaching is increasingly widespread in organizations, there is still work to be done in understanding what is behind the rapid growth of coaching, how and why organizations use coaching and what they are learning from the experience.

A couple of years ago the UK-based Institute of Leadership and Management (ILM) published a research report entitled 'Creating a Coaching Culture'. It revealed that most organizations using coaching adopt it as part of their overall approach to learning and development. Furthermore, organizations report that coaching delivers a number of benefits above and beyond the initial objectives.

Today we shall look at ways of ensuring that coaching becomes an integral part of people management and development in our organizations.

The business case for coaching skills

We might argue that coaching, like motherhood and apple pie, is a good thing by definition. Good coaching promises considerable benefits, including improved productivity, focused development, improved morale and more cohesive teams.

However, as with most people-development initiatives, coaching outcomes are difficult to quantify in the same way that we evaluate, say, the introduction of a new IT system.

Nevertheless, most organizations rightly demand a strong rationale for introducing coaching to their people-development frameworks, particularly where this incurs costs in time and money for training managers and team leaders in coaching skills.

The arguments *for* introducing coaching

We have to deal with constant change

At one time we could expect to leave school, college or university with an education that would last our working life. We could enter the workplace and refine and develop this knowledge. As we moved up the ladder and into supervisory or managerial positions, we could impart our knowledge and expertise and share our wisdom with those who would eventually replace us. Knowledge was power and commanded respect. Managers would proudly say, 'I wouldn't ask anybody to do anything I'm unable to do myself.'

This position is no longer sustainable. It is estimated that the body of knowledge we have when we leave the education sector is redundant inside three years. Managers cannot hope to keep pace with the ins and outs of all the jobs performed by their teams. It would be like trying to nail jelly to a wall.

Coaching, with its emphasis on drawing out rather than putting in, emerges as the only way of leading and developing people in our increasingly dynamic and fluid workplaces.

We work in flatter structures

During the 1990s and early 2000s increasing competition and developments in technology, among other things, meant that many organizations underwent some kind of 'downsizing'. More often than not this meant losing large numbers of so-called middle managers. This resulted in the managers left behind having to find ways of achieving more results with fewer resources.

Where previously organizations would have carried some slack, there was now a need to be precise and focused in all areas of activity. Vertical reporting lines were abandoned in favour of matrix management. People could expect to report to two or three managers, depending on the work they were doing. Technology took care of more of the routine tasks and people were free to work on business development in project teams, with a high need for creative thinking.

This is still the case today and will be even more so in the future. Against this background, managers cannot hope to lead and develop their teams by being the font of all knowledge and simply passing down the orders. Instead, we need ways to help people access their creativity and flair. We need to make people feel empowered, resourceful and motivated to achieve. Coaching offers a practical way of achieving these aims.

People are the only true competitive advantage

If we get a new IT system or piece of plant, our competitors can get the same by the following week. We might secure a large amount of capital investment or funding but there would be nothing to stop our competitors doing the same.

Any organization, however sophisticated, is ultimately a collection of people. It follows that, if we want to improve business performance, we must always look to improve the performance of individuals and teams. This is where the potential for improvement lies.

It is frustrating to hear senior managers cry, 'We have got to get the best *out of* people,' and then watch as they do the exact opposite and spend a fortune on various ways of stuffing the best *into* people. Coaching provides the antidote to this approach.

People expect to be developed

The essential 'deal' of working for an organization has changed irreversibly. Once we could expect security and a job for life in return for our valiant efforts at work. Now we cannot expect to remain in a job for life, whatever our level of performance.

The new 'deal' is that, in return for our work and endeavours, we expect to grow and to be developed. Then we might move on to bigger and better things and perhaps to a different organization. People now talk of CV building and employability as being crucial areas to consider.

Coaching can deliver on these expectations and it can do so quickly. It can help organizations provide the development that people expect, without the huge investment required for complex training programmes.

The arguments *against* introducing coaching

Despite the compelling reasons that we might offer for introducing coaching, we can expect to encounter many barriers. We need to understand what these barriers are and how we might help others develop their understanding of coaching so that these barriers can be removed.

We have got enough on our plate as it is

Most organizations seem to be working at the edge of chaos. Change is abundant and managers are rightly worried that one more change will prove to be 'the straw that breaks the camel's back'. Seen in this way, coaching, as just one more stand-alone initiative, is bound to take a back seat. However, coaching should not be seen in this way. Coaching can be the glue that binds change initiative together. After all, we know that all change programmes have a *people* element. If staff and other stakeholders are not carefully guided through the changes, failure is quite likely.

When managers are equipped with good coaching skills, they are able to help their staff to understand both the underlying reasons for change and the unsettling feelings that result. More importantly, managers who coach will be able to empower their teams to find their own coping strategies, rather than crowbar them into prescriptive methods that usually provoke rebellion rather than commitment.

Now is not the right time

If people are claiming this then, paradoxically, it is absolutely the right time for coaching. Good, effective coaching raises awareness, generates responsibility and builds trust. There is never any sense in delaying the use of these qualities.

If we leave coaching until 'other things have settled down', it is like saying that we shall put the umbrellas up once it has stopped raining.

It will cost too much

Much depends on how the costs are calculated. There is an upfront investment of time and money to train managers and team leaders as coaches. However, this can be saved over and over again by the consequent improvements in team performance. Compare the cost of one manager receiving coaching training so that he or she can help the team members become effective at personal organization with the cost of sending a whole team on time-management courses.

Deciding whether we should implement coaching in an organization can be compared with clearing a forest. Do we stop, from time to time, to sharpen the axe and thus clear the forest more quickly and effectively in the end? Or do we keep hacking away with a blunt blade so that we can 'just get to the end of this next tree'?

How to implement coaching

We now need to take a practical stance and think about how we might actually introduce coaching in our workplaces. The following version of the coaching ARROW includes some specific questions on this very issue to help us decide how to do this. You could either work through them for yourself or, better still, get someone else to coach you.

 TIP *Remember that your primary concerns are to raise awareness, generate responsibility and build trust with the people you coach.*

Aims

- What are you trying to achieve by introducing coaching?
- What do you see as the benefits?
- What are the risks of not having coaching?
- What specific outcomes do you want?
- Are they challenging but achievable?
- How will you know if you have succeeded?
- What time frame is involved?

Reality

- How clear are you about your organization's performance goals?
- How effective are managers at developing people?
- To what extent are people prepared to take risks?
- How does your organization view mistakes?
- What have you tried so far?
- What results did you get?

Reflection

- How big is the gap between aims and reality?
- How realistic are your aims?
- Is coaching required?
- What else might be required?
- What is the focus of the coaching?
- Who will it be for?

Options

- What could you do about all this?
- What else could you try?
- What would you do if you had more time or money or authority?
- Whose advice could you seek?
- What suggestions would they have?
- What would you do if you knew you couldn't fail?
- Would you like another suggestion?

Way forward

- What exactly are you going to do?
- When are you going to do it?
- Who needs to know?
- Will you use internal or external coaches?
- How will you train them?
- What are the communication requirements?
- Who will manage the project?
- How will you monitor and evaluate the project?
- What is your commitment to this course of action on a scale of 1–10?

As always, we must look upon the questions only as a means to promote good-quality thinking, to raise our *awareness* of our current situation and to show how we might move forward. There is no magic formula for implementing coaching. That *responsibility* is yours.

Final thought

As we complete this short journey through the fascinating and emerging world of coaching, we can perhaps keep its true purpose close to our hearts by considering that the term 'coach' is an old French word meaning 'to transport important people from one place to another'.

Summary of the week

This week we have covered a lot of ground in a short time. On Sunday we saw that coaching requires a positive view of people in the workplace and that it needs to be considered alongside other development methods.

On Monday we looked at how coaching fits into management roles and how it enables us to use a flexible communication approach ranging from *Tells* to *Delegates*. On Tuesday we examined the principles underpinning effective coaching.

On Wednesday and Thursday we explored the coaching ARROW model as a way of applying a structure to coaching questions, enabling the people we coach to move from vague thoughts to specific actions. On Friday we looked at coaching in context and how we must consider aspects of our organizational culture before we embark on coaching.

Finally, today we developed a business case for coaching and saw that it offers a means of dealing with a range of workplace issues, such as organizational development and managing change.

Fact-check [answers at the back]

1. Which of these reasons is not part of the business case for coaching skills?
a) Improved productivity ❑
b) Focused development ❑
c) Improved morale ❑
d) The latest trend ❑

2. The proud management boast of, 'I wouldn't ask anybody to do anything I'm not able to do myself' is...
a) Arrogant ❑
b) Silly ❑
c) No longer sustainable ❑
d) To be admired ❑

3. What makes people feel empowered at work?
a) More money ❑
b) More status ❑
c) Responsibility and support ❑
d) A big enough threat ❑

4. What do senior managers who cry, 'We have to get the best out of our people!' then often do?
a) Nothing ❑
b) Try to do the opposite ❑
c) Implement the coaching approach ❑
d) Have a meeting ❑

5. How can we respond to the objection of 'We've got enough on our plate as it is'?
a) 'You think you're busy? Try working in our department!' ❑
b) 'Don't come to us with problems, come with solutions.' ❑
c) 'Why are you always so negative?' ❑
d) 'Coaching is not *another* change, it's about *dealing* with change.' ❑

6. How can we respond to the objection of 'It will cost too much'?
a) 'We're all having to cope with tight budgets.' ❑
b) 'Surely you can make savings elsewhere?' ☑
c) 'Coaching is an investment. We can show that the costs are recoverable.' ❑
d) 'Why are you always so negative?' ❑

7. How can we respond to the objection of 'Our team leaders are highly skilled anyway'?
a) 'Oh, no, they're not.' ❑
b) 'Yes, they are. And when they can coach, they'll be even more so.' ❑
c) 'Yeah, right.' ❑
d) 'But if we teach them to coach too, what harm can it do?' ❑

8. What do people expect from the new 'deal' at work in return for their work and endeavours?
a) To grow and be developed ❏
b) To retire early on a fat pension ❏
c) To sit back and let the promotions come ❏
d) To remain in the job for life ❏

9. What is an organization's true competitive advantage?
a) Branding, because consumers respond to glossy logos ❏
b) Plant and machinery, because who else could have such fine resources? ❏
c) People, because in the end their skills and attitudes are the only thing that can't be replicated ❏
d) People, because we pay more than our rivals ❏

10. Why is implementing coaching a bit like clearing a forest?
a) You can't see the wood for the trees ❏
b) You sometimes have to stop and sharpen your axe ❏
c) It is a largely thankless task ❏
d) Just hacking away at it is likely to be good enough ❏

7 × 7

Seven great coaching quotes

1 'Knowledge speaks, but wisdom listens.' Jimi Hendrix (1942–70), guitarist and songwriter
2 'Trying fails, awareness cures.' Fritz Perls (1893–1970), German-born psychotherapist
3 'Tell me what you want, what you really, really want.' Spice Girls
4 'High performers are simply people that learn faster.' Peter Block (1940–), author and consultant
5 'The mind is key, but who holds the key to your mind?' Sir John Whitmore (1937–), racing driver and eminent business coach
6 'Performance is equal to potential minus interference.' Timothy Gallwey (1938–), author and pioneer of modern business coaching
7 'In the future, those who are not coaches will not be promoted.' Jack Welch (1935–), former CEO, General Electric

Seven things coaching is most definitely about

1 Drawing out, not putting in. As coaches, our starting position should be that people come pre-packed with what they need to succeed. Our job is not to stuff them full of our own ideas and experiences but instead to draw out of them an awareness of what holds them back.
2 Helping others to learn as opposed to teaching them things. In a similar vein, our role is to create the conditions in which people can learn rather than insist that they absorb our wisdom.
3 Being motivating and enjoyable. Done well, coaching should be a welcome use of time for both coach and coachee.
4 Being performance-focused but people-centred. Coaching at work is about getting the best performance that we can, but it also recognizes that it is living, breathing human beings, not machines, that ultimately produce results.

5 Releasing potential. We start from the idea that people have what they need and we work to help identify and overcome barriers to such potential being expressed.

6 Creating independence. As our coaching works and people grow in confidence and competence they become less reliant on us and more able to accept new challenges.

7 Helping people move out of their comfort zones. Above all, it's about helping people grow and develop, and to do this we must also challenge and push, albeit in an atmosphere of high support.

Seven things coaching is most definitely *not* about

1 Telling people what to do – because telling someone what to do does not necessarily enable them to be able to do it.

2 Instructing, training or counselling. While coaching is often spoken about at the same time as these things, it is a very particular way of developing people, as we have seen.

3 Offering uninvited feedback – which normally causes people to find all sorts of reasons to not accept the feedback

4 Rescuing people and having all the answers. As managers, we cannot always have the answer, and some work situations are unique and need to be addressed as such.

5 Only for poor performers. Sometimes coaching has its most dramatic effect when used with someone who is already doing quite well but has so much more to give.

6 A cosy chat – this is the last thing any of us have time for!

7 A disciplinary measure. If coaching is seen in this way, it is unlikely that anyone being coached will communicate honestly enough to make it worth while.

Seven great coaching resources

1 Tim Gallwey, *The Inner Game of Tennis* (Jonathan Cape, 1975). Many consider Gallwey the father of modern coaching. While the concepts outlined here were discovered on the tennis court, they are applicable to any coaching situation in a work setting.

2 John Whitmore, *Coaching for Performance* (Nicholas Brealey, 1994). Alongside Gallwey, Whitmore pioneered many of the coaching techniques we now consider commonplace. This book closed the gap between coaching in sport and coaching at work and demonstrated how powerful the GROW questioning sequence could be in a work setting.

3 Nancy Klein, *Time to Think* (Cassell, 2002). Not a book on coaching techniques as such but a deep examination of the part that listening plays in working with people to dismantle their limiting beliefs. Applied carefully, Klein's ideas can take a simple coaching conversation to a whole new level.

4 Daniel Pink, *Drive* (Canongate Books, 2011). A deconstruction of a whole range of myths around the nature of motivation in the modern world which shows how misguided it can be to rely on external rewards and pay and sets out the case for focusing instead on the enduring internal motivators of autonomy, mastery and purpose.

5 www.associationforcoaching.com. First formed in the UK but now with global coverage, the Association for Coaching is leading the way as the professional body for coaches, be they independent practitioners or work-based managers and leaders.

6 www.businessballs.com. A website containing an amazing array of exercises and models that coaches can use to help their coachees develop.

7 www.mindtools.com. The app versions for both IOS and Android provide an invaluable on the spot resource to pick up themes and ideas uncovered in a coaching conversation and examine them further.

Seven signs that you are moving towards a coaching culture

1 In a coaching culture the stories people tell are about success. There is no awkwardness or false modesty and tales of people doing well are shared widely and enthusiastically.

2 The routines and rituals in a coaching culture are about people and performance. An organization that has committed to regular performance reviews for all staff and that holds

pre- and post-learning-event discussions, for example, has clearly identified these routines as important.

3 The structures at play in a coaching culture would tend to be flatter with an emphasis on innovation and collaborative working rather than reinforcing a hierarchy.

4 Similarly, there would be fewer control systems in a coaching culture than elsewhere. The emphasis instead is on the key coaching principles of trust and responsibility.

5 In a coaching culture power would centre around those who can get results through others. Position power or expert power would be used sparingly.

6 A coaching culture plays down the symbols of individual status such as fancy job titles and expensive office suites and instead promotes the symbols of shared success such as team reward programmes and celebration events.

7 Perhaps the greatest indicator, though, of coaching culture is in the day-to-day behaviour of the senior leadership team. Unless this embraces the principles of coaching in deed as well as in word, coaching will be unlikely to take root in the long term.

Seven tips for coaching difficult people

1 Look for the cause. We don't generally recruit known cynics or troublemakers so, if someone is proving to be a difficult employee, the first step might be to understand what has happened in their view to cause this behaviour.

2 Deal with the performance, not the person. This is a great trick if you can pull it off, though it is not easy in emotional situations: try to deal with what the person *does* rather than get tangled up in the sort of person they *are*.

3 Be descriptive not evaluative. When giving feedback, offer your observations of what actually happened and the consequences rather than judging things as good, bad or otherwise. People can't argue with the facts but they can argue against your judgements.

4 Don't comment on attitude. Attitude must be the most subjective term used at work. Every one of us believes that our own attitude is useful and appropriate or we would change it, so

telling someone that they have the wrong attitude is pointless. Describing what they did and the results that ensued will prove much more productive.

5 Deal with things in private. At some stage you and your difficult employee are going to need to have a conversation. This must absolutely be done in private if you are to have any chance of getting back on an even keel. Many of the previous tips are designed to help you avoid storing things up until you lose your temper and blurt out your frustrations in front of everybody.

6 Consider the wider team. As Mr Spock used to say in *Star Trek*, 'The needs of the many outweigh the needs of the few and of the one.' When we have difficulties with one member of staff, it can be easy for them to soak up all our energy and attention and for us to neglect our other team members.

7 Don't sweep problems under the carpet. There's no point placing the problem person in some half-baked project role or inventing some other non-job to get them out of the way. Small businesses simply can't accommodate the costs of this tactic and large organizations should think carefully about the messages this sends.

Seven ways to make coaching stick

1 Follow up initial training. While a typical one- or two-day coaching skills training course will equip managers with the basic tools and techniques, it will address only a change in *behaviour*. Where behavioural change is not accompanied by a similar change in thinking and attitude, it will not stick. A series of follow-ups to any initial training is useful, particularly where the participants are required to be coached on an ongoing work issue and to regularly report back on their progress.

2 Include a coaching module on all 'people skills' training. In order to move away from coaching as 'task' to coaching as 'style', it must be seen as part of the overall approach to managing people. It is therefore useful to reflect this need in all people skills training and not just specific coaching workshops.

3 Get the support of the most senior person you can. Where coaching is seen as merely a skill to learn, the involvement of the training department is all that is required. However, where coaching is seen – as it should be – as part of organizational

and cultural change, it becomes a policy decision that requires the full support of the senior team. However, it is not necessary to get the whole team on board from the start: target the most obvious champion and work from there.

4 Coach the senior team so that they get the benefits. Many of my coaching skills training projects had their seed in a senior executive being bowled over by the benefits of being coached and wanting that experience to permeate throughout the organization.

5 Make sure that high performers are coached, too. Too often, coaching is seen as remedial and people understandably shy away from being seen as needing 'special lessons'. We can overcome this through coaching by stealth – that is, by not labelling it as such – though this seems counterproductive if we are really trying to increase the take-up of coaching. An alternative is very deliberately to coach those who are already high-performers. They are highly likely to welcome the initiative and become strong advocates for the approach.

6 Share coaching success stories loudly and visibly. As above, the positive aspects of coaching should be shouted from the rooftops as much as possible.

7 Include a coaching-related key performance indicator (KPI) in managers' performance reviews. 'What gets measured gets done', so the saying goes, so if we really want managers to give as much energy and attention to people and well as task matters, we should measure their results with equal seriousness

Answers

Sunday: 1c; 2a; 3a; 4d; 5b; 6b; 7d; 8b; 9b; 10a

Monday: 1d; 2c; 3a; 4b; 5c; 6b; 7b; 8b; 9c; 10d

Tuesday: 1b; 2b; 3c; 4b; 5b; 6c; 7d; 8b; 9a; 10b

Wednesday: 1b; 2b; 3d; 4a; 5a; 6d; 7b; 8d; 9c; 10a

Thursday: 1b; 2a; 3b; 4c; 5d; 6d; 7c; 8a; 9c; 10a

Friday: 1c; 2d; 3c; 4d; 5c; 6b; 7c; 8b; 9a; 10b

Saturday: 1d; 2c; 3c; 4b; 5d; 6c; 7b; 8a; 9c; 10b